Fix-It and Forget-It

MEDITERRANEAN DIET
Cookbook

7-INGREDIENT HEALTHY INSTANT POT AND SLOW COOKER MEALS

HOPE COMERFORD

Good Books
New York, New York

To my amazing music students . . . you inspire me every day. I love the enthusiasm and encouragement you give me every time we are together. Thank you for making music and memories with me! The future is a bright, bright place with the prospect of *you* in it!

Contents

Welcome to *Fix-It and Forget-It Mediterranean Diet Cookbook*

Renowned for its amazing health benefits, such as lowering cholesterol, weight loss, anti-inflammatory properties, improving heart health, increasing energy, and much more, the Mediterranean diet is quickly gaining popularity. It's not really a "diet" but rather a method of eating just the right ingredients. To follow a Mediterranean diet, one focuses on whole grains, beans, plant-based proteins, fish, vegetables, fruits, nuts, seeds, spices, and, of course, olive oil. Moderate amounts of dairy, poultry and eggs are allowed, and red meat is not recommended.

This book is unique because I've put together recipes that you can easily throw together with seven main ingredients or fewer. Below, you will find a list of Mediterranean pantry staples you will always want to have plenty of on hand for the recipes in this book, as they are not included in the seven-ingredient recipe count. Don't worry, these are mainly spices and a few other Mediterranean diet "must-haves." Everything else you need for each recipe will be listed in a handy grocery list on each recipe page.

I want to thank you for taking your health into your own hands by preparing delicious and healthy food for you and your family! While home cooking takes a bit more effort, with a little planning and a smidge of preparation, you will not only be successful, but feel proud and accomplished! Best of luck on your Mediterranean diet journey! Now get that pantry set up and get cooking!

What Qualifies as a Seven-Ingredient Recipe?

- A recipe that has seven or fewer ingredients.
- Spices do not count.
- Water does not count.
- Items listed under "Mediterranean Pantry Staples" do not count.
- *Optional* ingredients do not count.
- Serving suggestion items, such as rice, whole-grain pasta, etc. do not count.

Mediterranean Diet Pantry Staples

The following are ingredients that are very common in the Mediterranean diet. These are items you will consistently need for the recipes in this cookbook. If you always keep these items on hand, you'll just need a few more ingredients for each recipe. These items will appear in the "grocery list" for each recipe in this cookbook in order to simplify things for you!

- Ancho chile powder
- Bay leaves
- Basil, dried
- Black pepper
- Cayenne pepper
- Celery seed
- Chili powder
- Chives, dried
- Cinnamon, ground
- Cloves, ground
- Coriander, ground
- Cumin
- Curry powder
- Coconut oil
- Garam masala
- Garlic, fresh cloves
- Garlic powder
- Ginger, ground
- Herbes de Provence
- Honey
- Italian seasoning
- Lemon pepper seasoning
- Marjoram
- No-salt seasoning
- Nutmeg, ground
- Olive oil
- Onion flakes
- Onion powder
- Onions (yellow, white, red, sweet)
- Oregano, dried
- Paprika
- Parsley flakes
- Poultry seasoning
- Red pepper
- Red pepper flakes
- Rosemary, dried
- Sage, dried
- Salt (table, sea, kosher)
- Seasoned salt
- Thyme
- Turmeric
- Vegetable broth
- Vegetable stock

Choosing a Slow Cooker

Not all slow cookers are created equal . . . or work equally as well for everyone!

Those of us who use slow cookers frequently know we have our own preferences when it comes to which slow cooker we choose to use. For instance, I love my programmable slow cooker, but there are many programmable slow cookers I've tried that I've strongly disliked. Why? Because some go by increments of 15 or 30 minutes, and some go by 4, 6, 8, or 10 hours. I dislike those restrictions, but I have family and friends who don't mind them at all! I am also pretty brand loyal when it comes to my manual slow cookers because I've had great success with those and have had unsuccessful moments with slow cookers of other brands. So, which slow cooker(s) is/are best for your household?

It really depends on how many people you're feeding and if you're gone for long periods of time. Here are my recommendations:

For 2–3 person household	3–5 quart slow cooker
For 4–5 person household	5–6 quart slow cooker
For a 6+ person household	6½–7 quart slow cooker

Large slow cooker advantages/disadvantages:

Advantages:
- You can fit a loaf pan or a baking dish into a 6- or 7-qt., depending on the shape of your cooker. That allows you to make bread or cakes, or even smaller quantities of main dishes. (Take your favorite baking dish and loaf pan along when you shop for a cooker to make sure they'll fit inside.)
- You can feed large groups of people, or make larger quantities of food, allowing for leftovers, or meals, to freeze.

Disadvantages:
- They take up more storage room.
- They don't fit as neatly into a dishwasher.
- If your crock isn't ⅔–¾ full, you may burn your food.

Small slow cooker advantages/disadvantages:

Advantages:
- They're great for lots of appetizers, for serving hot drinks, for baking cakes straight in the crock, and for dorm rooms or apartments.
  Great option for making recipes of smaller quantities.

Disadvantages:

- Food in smaller quantities tends to cook more quickly than larger amounts. So keep an eye on it.
- Chances are, you won't have many leftovers. So, if you like to have leftovers, a smaller slow cooker may not be a good option for you.

My recommendation:

Have at least two slow cookers; one around 3 to 4 qt. and one 6 qt. or larger. A third would be a huge bonus (and a great advantage to your cooking repertoire). The advantage of having at least a couple is you can make a larger variety of recipes. Also, you can make at least two or three dishes at once for a whole meal.

Manual vs. Programmable

If you are gone for only six to eight hours a day, a manual slow cooker might be just fine for you. If you are gone for more than eight hours during the day, I would highly recommend purchasing a programmable slow cooker that will switch to warm when the cook time you set is up. It will allow you to cook a wider variety of recipes.

The two I use most frequently are my 4-qt. manual slow cooker and my 6½-qt. programmable slow cooker. I like that I can make smaller portions in my 4-qt. slow cooker on days I don't need or want leftovers, but I also love how my 6½-qt. slow cooker can accommodate whole chickens, turkey breasts, hams, or big batches of soups. I use them both often.

Get to know your slow cooker . . .

Plan a little time to get acquainted with your slow cooker. Each slow cooker has its own personality—just like your oven (and your car). Plus, many new slow cookers cook hotter and faster than earlier models. I think that with all of the concern for food safety, the slow-cooker manufacturers have amped up their settings so that "High," "Low," and "Warm" are all higher temperatures than in the older models. That means they cook hotter—and therefore, faster— than the first slow cookers. The beauty of these little machines is that they're supposed to cook low and slow. We count on that when we flip the switch in the morning before we leave the house for ten hours or so. So, because none of us knows what kind of temperament our slow cooker has until we try it out, nor how hot it cooks—don't assume anything. Save yourself a disappointment and make the first recipe in your new slow cooker on a day when you're at home. Cook it for the shortest amount of time the recipe calls for. Then, check the food to see if it's done. Or if you start smelling food that seems to be finished, turn off the cooker and rescue your food.

Also, all slow cookers seem to have a "hot spot," which is of great importance to know, especially when baking with your slow cooker. This spot may tend to burn food in that area if you're not careful. If you're baking directly in your slow cooker, I recommend covering the "hot spot" with some foil.

Take notes . . .

Don't be afraid to make notes in your cookbook. It's yours! Chances are, it will eventually get passed down to someone in your family and they will love and appreciate all of your musings. Take note of which slow cooker you used and exactly how long it took to cook the recipe. The next time you make it, you won't need to try to remember. Apply what you learned to the next recipes you make in your cooker. If another recipe says it needs to cook for 7 to 9 hours, and you've discovered your slow cooker cooks on the faster side, cook that recipe for 6 to 6½ hours and then check it. You can always cook a recipe longer—but you can't reverse things if it's overdone.

Get creative . . .

If you know your morning is going to be hectic, prepare everything the night before, take it out so the crock warms up to room temperature when you first get up in the morning, then plug it in and turn it on as you're leaving the house.

If you want to make something that has a short cook time and you're going to be gone longer than that, cook it the night before and refrigerate it for the next day. Warm it up when you get home. Or, cook those recipes on the weekend when you know you'll be home and eat them later in the week.

Slow-Cooking Tips and Tricks and Other Things You May Not Know

* Slow cookers tend to work best when they're ⅔ to ¾ of the way full. You may need to increase the cooking time if you've exceeded that amount, or reduce it if you've put in less than that. If you're going to exceed that limit, it would be best to reduce the recipe, or split it between two slow cookers. (Remember how I suggested owning at least two or three slow cookers?)

- Keep your veggies on the bottom. That puts them in more direct contact with the heat. The fuller your slow cooker, the longer it will take its contents to cook. Also, the more densely packed the cooker's contents are, the longer they will take to cook. And finally, the larger the chunks of meat or vegetables, the more time they will need to cook.

- Keep the lid on! Every time you take a peek, you lose 20 minutes of cooking time. Please take this into consideration each time you lift the lid! I know, some of you can't help yourselves and are going to lift anyway. Just don't forget to tack on 20 minutes to your cook time for each time you peeked!

- Sometimes it's beneficial to remove the lid. If you'd like your dish to thicken a bit, take the lid off during the last half hour to hour of cooking time.

- If you have a big slow cooker (7- to 8-qt.), you can cook a small batch in it by putting the recipe ingredients into an oven-safe baking dish or baking pan and then placing that into the cooker's crock. First, put a trivet or some metal jar rings on the bottom of the crock, and then set your dish or pan on top of them. Or a loaf pan may "hook onto" the top ridges of the crock belonging to a large oval cooker and hang there straight and securely, "baking" a cake or quick bread. Cover the cooker and flip it on.

- The outside of your slow cooker will be hot! Please remember to keep it out of reach of children and keep that in mind for yourself as well!

- Get yourself a quick-read meat thermometer and use it! This helps remove the question of whether or not your meat is fully cooked, and helps prevent you from overcooking your meat as well.
  - Internal Cooking Temperatures: Beef—125–130°F (rare); 140–145°F (medium); 160°F (well-done)
  - Pork—140–145°F (rare); 145–150°F (medium); 160°F (well-done)
  - Turkey and Chicken—165°F
  - Frozen meat: The basic rule of thumb is, don't put frozen meat into the slow cooker. The meat does not reach the proper internal temperature in time. This especially applies to thick cuts of meat! Proceed with caution!

- Add fresh herbs 10 minutes before the end of the cooking time to maximize their flavor.

- If your recipe calls for cooked pasta, add it 10 minutes before the end of the cooking time if the cooker is on High; 30 minutes before the end of the cooking time if it's on Low. Then the pasta won't get mushy.

- If your recipe calls for sour cream or cream, stir it in 5 minutes before the end of the cooking time. You want it to heat but not boil or simmer.
  - Approximate Slow-Cooker Temperatures (Remember, each slow cooker is different): High—212°F–300°F

- Low—170°F–200°F
- Simmer—185°F
- Warm—165°F
- Cooked and dried bean measurements: 16-ounce can, drained = about 1¾ cups beans
  - 19-ounce can, drained = about 2 cups beans
  - 1 lb. dried beans (about 2½ cups) = 5 cups cooked beans

Getting Started with Your Instant Pot

What is an Instant Pot?

In short, and Instant Pot is a digital pressure cooker that also has multiple other functions. Not only can it be used as a pressure cooker, but depending on which model Instant Pot you have, you can set it to do things like sauté, cook rice, multigrains, porridge, soup/stew, beans/chili, porridge, meat, poultry, cake, eggs, yogurt, steam, slow cook or even set it manually. Because the Instant Pot has so many functions, it takes away the need for multiple appliances on your counter and uses less pots and pans.

Get to know your Instant Pot . . .

The very first thing most Instant Pot owners do is called the water test. It helps you get to know your Instant Pot a bit, familiarizes you with it, and might even take a bit of your apprehension away (because if you're anything like me, I was scared to death to use it!).

Step 1: Plug in your Instant Pot. This may seem obvious to some, but when we're nervous about using a new appliance, sometimes we forget things like this.
Step 2: Make sure the inner pot is inserted in the cooker. You should NEVER attempt to cook anything in your device without the inner pot, or you will ruin your Instant Pot. Food should never come into contact with the actual housing unit.
Step 3: The inner pot has lines for each cup (how convenient, right?!). Fill the inner pot with water until it reaches the 3-cup line.
Step 4: Check the sealing ring to be sure it's secure and in place. You should not be able to move it around. If it's not in place properly, you may experience issues with the pot letting out a lot of steam while cooking, or not coming to pressure.
Step 5: Seal the lid. There is an arrow on the lid between and "open" and "close." There is also an arrow on the top of the base of the Instant Pot between a picture of a locked lock and an unlocked lock. Line those arrows up, then turn the lid toward the picture of the lock (left.) You

will hear a noise that will indicate the lid is locked. If you do not hear a noise, it's not locked. Try it again.

Step 6: *Always* check to see if the steam valve on top of the lid is turned to "sealing." If it's not on "sealing" and is on "venting," it will not be able to come to pressure.

Step 7: Press the "Steam" button and use the +/- arrow to set it to 2 minutes. Once it's at the desired time, you don't need to press anything else. In a few seconds, the Instant Pot will begin all on its own. For those of us with digital slow cookers, we have a tendency to look for the "start" button, but there isn't one on the Instant Pot.

Step 8: Now you wait for the "magic" to happen! The "cooking" will begin once the device comes to pressure. This can take anywhere from 5 to 30 minutes, I've found in my experience. Then, you will see the countdown happen (from the time you set it at). After that, the Instant Pot will beep, which means your meal is done!

Step 9: Your Instant Pot will now automatically switch to "warm" and begin a count of how many minutes it's been on warm. The next part is where you either wait for the NPR, or natural pressure release (meaning the pressure releases all on its own), or you do what's called a QR, or quick release (meaning, you manually release the pressure). Which method you choose depends on what you're cooking, but in this case, you can choose either since it's just water. For NPR, you will wait for the lever to move all the way back over to "venting" and watch the pinion (float valve) next to the lever. It will be flush with the lid when at full pressure and will drop when the pressure is done releasing. If you choose QR, be very careful not to have your hands over the vent as the steam is very hot and you can burn yourself.

The Three Most Important Buttons You Need to Know About . . .

You will find the majority of recipes will use the following three buttons:

Manual/Pressure Cook: Some older models tend to say "Manual" and the newer models seem to say "Pressure Cook." They mean the same thing. From here, you use the +/- button to change the cook time. After several seconds, the Instant Pot will begin its process. The exact name of this button will vary depending on your model of Instant Pot.

Sauté: Many recipes will have you sauté vegetables or brown meat before beginning the pressure cooking process. For this setting, you will not use the lid of the Instant Pot.

Keep Warm/Cancel: This may just be the most important button on the Instant Pot. When you forget to use the +/- buttons to change the time for a recipe, or you press a wrong button, you can hit "keep warm/cancel" and it will turn your Instant Pot off for you.

What Do All the Buttons Do?

With so many buttons, it's hard to remember what each one does or means. You can use this as a quick guide in a pinch.

Soup/Broth. This button cooks at high pressure for 30 minutes. It can be adjusted using the +/- buttons to cook more for 40 minutes, or less for 20 minutes.

Meat/Stew. This button cooks at high pressure for 35 minutes. It can be adjusted using the +/- buttons to cook more for 45 minutes, or less for 20 minutes.

Bean/Chili. This button cooks at high pressure for 30 minutes. It can be adjusted using the +/- buttons to cook more for 40 minutes, or less for 25 minutes.

Poultry. This button cooks at high pressure for 15 minutes. It can be adjusted using the +/- buttons to cook more 30 minutes, or less for 5 minutes.

Rice. This button cooks at low pressure and is the only fully automatic program. It is for cooking white rice and will automatically adjust the cooking time depending on the amount of water and rice in the cooking pot.

Multigrain. This button cooks at high pressure for 40 minutes. It can be adjusted using the +/- buttons to cook more for 45 minutes of warm-water soaking time and 60 minutes pressure-cooking time, or less for 20 minutes.

Porridge. This button cooks at high pressure for 20 minutes. It can be adjusted using the +/- buttons to cook more for 30 minutes or less for 15 minutes.

Steam. This button cooks at high pressure for 10 minutes. It can be adjusted using the +/- buttons to cook more for 15 minutes, or less for 3 minutes. Always use a rack or steamer basket with this function, because it heats at full power continuously while it's coming to pressure and you do not want food in direct contact with the bottom of the pressure cooking pot or it will burn. Once it reaches pressure, the steam button regulates pressure by cycling on and off, similar to the other pressure buttons.

Less | Normal | More. Adjust between the *Less | Normal | More* settings by pressing the same cooking function button repeatedly until you get to the desired setting. (Older versions use the *Adjust* button.)

+/- Buttons. Adjust the cook time up [+] or down [-]. (On newer models, you can also press and hold [-] or [+] for 3 seconds to turn sound OFF or ON.)

Cake. This button cooks at high pressure for 30 minutes. It can be adjusted using the +/- buttons to cook more for 40 minutes, or less for 25 minutes.

Egg. This button cooks at high pressure for 5 minutes. It can be adjusted using the +/- buttons to cook more for 6 minutes, or less for 4 minutes.

Instant Pot Tips and Tricks and Other Things You May Not Know

- Never attempt to cook directly in the Instant Pot without the inner pot!
- Once you set the time, you can walk away. It will show the time you set it to, then will change to the word "on" while the pressure builds. Once the Instant Pot has come to pressure, you will once again see the time you set it for. It will count down from there.
- Always make sure your sealing ring is securely in place. If it shows signs of wear or tear, it needs to be replaced.
- Have a sealing ring for savory recipes and a separate sealing ring for sweet recipes. Many people report of their desserts tasting like a roast (or another savory food) if they try to use the same sealing ring for all recipes.
- The stainless-steel rack (trivet) your Instant Pot comes with can used to keep food from being completely submerged in liquid, like baked potatoes or ground beef. It can also be used to set another pot on, for pot in pot cooking.
- If you use warm or hot liquid instead of cold liquid, you may need to adjust the cooking time, or your food may not come out done.
- Always double-check to see that the valve on the lid is set to "sealing" and not "venting" when you first lock the lid. This will save you from your Instant Pot not coming to pressure.
- Use Natural Pressure Release for tougher cuts of meat, recipes with high starch (like rice or grains), and recipes with a high volume of liquid. This means you let the Instant Pot naturally release pressure. The little bobbin will fall once pressure is released completely.
- Use Quick Release for more delicate cuts of meat and preparation of vegetables—like seafood, chicken breasts, and steaming vegetables. This means you manually turn the vent (being careful not to put your hand over the vent) to release the pressure. The little bobbin will fall once pressure is released completely.
- Make sure there is a clear pathway for the steam to release. The last thing you want is to ruin the bottom of your cupboards with all that steam.
- You *must* use liquid in your Instant Pot. The *minimum* amount of liquid you should have in your inner pot is ½ cup; however, most recipes work best with at least 1 cup.
- Do *not* overfill your Instant Pot! It should only be ½ full for rice or beans (food that expands greatly when cooked), or ⅔ of the way full for almost everything else. Do not fill it to the max filled line.

- In this book, the Cooking Time *does not* take into account the amount of time it will take your Instant Pot to come to pressure, or the amount of time it will take the Instant Pot to release pressure. Be aware of this when choosing a recipe to make.
- If your Instant Pot is not coming to pressure, it's usually because the sealing ring is not on properly, or the vent is not set to "sealing."
- The more liquid, or the colder the ingredients, the longer it will take for the Instant Pot to come to pressure.
- Always make sure that the Instant Pot is dry before inserting the inner pot, and make sure the inner pot is dry before inserting it into the Instant Pot.
- Doubling a recipe does not change the cook time, but instead it will take longer to come up to pressure.
- You do not always need to double the liquid when doubling a recipe. Depending on what you're making, more liquid may make your food too watery. Use your best judgment.

Slow Cooker	Instant Pot
Warm	Less or Low
Low	Normal or Medium
High	More or High

Breakfast

Breakfast Sausage Casserole

Kendra Dreps
Liberty, PA

Makes 8 servings

Prep. Time: 15 minutes ⚜ *Chilling Time: 8 hours* ⚜ *Cooking Time: 4 hours* ⚜ *Ideal slow-cooker size: 3-qt.*

1 lb. meatless sausage crumbles

6 eggs

2 cups nondairy milk

8 slices whole-grain or sprouted-grain bread, cubed

1 cup reduced-fat shredded cheddar cheese

1. In a nonstick skillet, brown and drain sausage.

2. Mix eggs and milk in a large bowl.

3. Stir in bread cubes, cheese, and sausage.

4. Place in greased slow cooker.

5. Refrigerate overnight.

6. Cook on Low for 4 hours.

Variation:

Use cubed cooked ham instead of sausage.

Non Pantry Staple Grocery List

1 lb. meatless sausage crumbles

6 eggs

2 cups nondairy milk

8 slices whole-grain or sprouted-grain bread

1 cup reduced-fat shredded cheddar cheese

Calories 358
Fat 22.2 g
Saturated Fat 7 g
Cholesterol 147 mg
Sodium 861 mg
Total Carbs 16 g
Fiber 4 g
Protein 27 g

Vegetarian Sausage and Sweet Pepper Hash

Hope Comerford
Clinton Township, MI

Makes 6–8 servings
Prep. Time: 10 minutes   ♣   Cooking Time: 6½ hours   ♣   Ideal slow-cooker size: 4-qt.

1 (14-oz.) package vegetarian Italian sausage, cut lengthwise, then into ½-inch pieces

16 ounces frozen diced potatoes

1½ cups sliced onion

3 bell peppers, sliced (color of your choice)

¼ cup olive oil

1 teaspoon sea salt

½ teaspoon pepper

½ teaspoon dried thyme

½ teaspoon dried parsley

½ cup nutritional yeast

1. Spray crock with vegan nonstick spray.

2. Place sausage, frozen potatoes, onion, and sliced peppers into crock.

3. Mix with the olive oil, salt, pepper, thyme, parsley, and nutritional yeast.

4. Cover and cook on Low for 6 hours.

Non Pantry Staple Grocery List
1 (14-oz.) package vegetarian Italian sausage
16 ounces frozen diced potatoes
3 bell peppers (colors of your choice)
Nutritional yeast

Calories 263
Fat 16 g
Saturated Fat 2 g
Cholesterol 0 mg
Sodium 658 mg
Total Carbs 19 g
Fiber 3 g
Protein 14 g

Good-Start Oatmeal

Barbara Forrester Landis
Lititz, PA

Makes 6 servings
Prep. Time: 10 minutes   ⚬   Cooking Time: 2½–6 hours   ⚬   Ideal slow-cooker size: 3-qt.

1 cup steel-cut oats
1 cup dried cranberries
1 cup walnuts
½ teaspoon kosher salt
1 tablespoon cinnamon
2 cups water
2 cups nondairy milk (almond, rice, etc.)

1. Combine all dry ingredients in crock. Stir well.

2. Add water and nondairy milk and stir.

3. Cover. Cook on High for 2½ hours, or on Low for 5 to 6 hours.

Non Pantry Staple Grocery List
1 cup steel-cut oats
1 cup dried cranberries
1 cup walnuts
2 cups nondairy milk

Calories 318
Fat 15 g
Saturated Fat 1 g
Cholesterol 0 mg
Sodium 216 mg
Total Carbs 39 g
Fiber 7 g
Protein 8 g

Fruit Breakfast Cobbler

Hope Comerford
Clinton Township, MI

Makes 4 servings
Prep. Time: 10 minutes ⚬ Cooking Time: 15–20 minutes ⚬ Setting: Steam and Sauté ⚬ Release: Manual

2 pears, chopped

2 sweet apples, chopped

2 peaches, diced

2 tablespoons honey

3 tablespoons coconut oil

1 teaspoon ground cinnamon

½ cup unsweetened shredded coconut

½ cup pecans, diced

2 tablespoons flaxseed

¼ cup oats

1. Place the pears, apples, and peaches in the inner pot of your Instant Pot, then top with the honey, coconut oil, and cinnamon. Lock lid and set vent to sealing.

2. Press Steam and set to 8 minutes.

3. When cook time is up, do a quick release. When lid is able to be removed, remove the fruit with a slotted spoon and place in a bowl. You want to leave the juices in the inner pot.

4. Set the Instant Pot to Sauté and put in the shredded coconut, pecan pieces, flaxseed, and oats. Stir them constantly, until the shredded coconut is lightly toasted.

5. Spoon the shredded coconut/oat mixture over the steamed fruit and enjoy.

Non Pantry Staple Grocery List
2 pears
2 sweet apples
2 peaches
½ cup unsweetened shredded coconut
½ cup pecans
2 tablespoons flaxseed
¼ cup oats

Calories 416
Fat 25 g
Saturated Fat 13 g
Cholesterol 0 mg
Sodium 4 mg
Total Carbs 50 g
Fiber 10 g
Protein 4 g

Apple Breakfast Cobbler

Anona M. Teel
Bangor, PA

Makes 8 servings
Prep. Time: 25 minutes   Cooking Time: 2–9 hours   Ideal slow-cooker size: 4- or 5-qt.

8 medium apples, cored, peeled, sliced

2 tablespoons honey

Dash cinnamon

Juice of 1 lemon

2 tablespoons coconut oil, melted

2 cups granola (see recipes on pgs. 29 and 31)

1. Combine ingredients in slow cooker.

2. Cover. Cook on Low for 7 to 9 hours (while you sleep!), or on High for 2 to 3 hours (after you're up in the morning).

Non Pantry Staple Grocery List
8 medium apples
1 lemon
Granola (see recipes on pgs. 29 and 31)

Calories 432
Fat 29 g
Saturated Fat 10 g
Cholesterol 0 mg
Sodium 6 mg
Total Carbs 44 g
Fiber 9 g
Protein 6 g

Almond Date Oatmeal

Audrey L. Kneer
Williamsfield, IL

Makes 8 servings
Cooking Time: 4–8 hours, or overnight   Ideal slow-cooker size: 3-qt.

2 cups dry rolled oats

½ cup granola (see recipes on pgs. 29 and 31)

½ cup almonds, chopped

¼ cup dates, chopped

4½ cups water

1. Combine all ingredients in slow cooker.

2. Cover and cook on Low for 4 to 8 hours, or overnight.

3. Serve with your choice of nondairy milk.

Non Pantry Staple Grocery List
2 cups dry rolled oats
Granola (see recipes on pgs. 29 and 31)
½ cup almonds
¼ cup dates

Calories 215
Fat 12 g
Saturated Fat 2 g
Cholesterol 0 mg
Sodium 6 mg
Total Carbs 20 g
Fiber 4 g
Protein 6 g

Apple Cinnamon Oatmeal

Hope Comerford
Clinton Township, MI

Makes 2–3 servings
Prep. Time: 5 minutes & Cooking Time: 7 hours & Ideal slow-cooker size: 2-qt.

½ cup steel-cut oats
2 cups unsweetened nondairy milk
1 small apple, peeled and diced
½ teaspoon vanilla extract
¼ teaspoon cinnamon

1. Spray crock with nonstick spray.

2. Place all ingredients into crock and stir lightly.

3. Cover and cook on Low for 7 hours.

Serving suggestion:
Add a bit of honey if you wish at time of serving.

Non Pantry Staple Grocery List
½ cup steel-cut oats
2 cups unsweetened nondairy milk
1 small apple
½ teaspoon vanilla extract

Calories 174
Fat 4 g
Saturated Fat 0 g
Cholesterol 0 mg
Sodium 107 mg
Total Carbs 29 g
Fiber 6 g
Protein 5 g

Triple Grain Breakfast

Cynthia Haller
New Holland, PA

Makes 4–5 servings
Prep. Time: 5 minutes   ⁂   Cooking Time: 3½ hours   ⁂   Ideal slow-cooker size: 4-qt.

⅓ cup uncooked quinoa
⅓ cup uncooked millet
⅓ cup uncooked brown rice
4 cups water
¼ teaspoon salt
½ cup raisins or dried cranberries
¼ cup chopped nuts, optional
1 teaspoon vanilla extract, optional
½ teaspoon ground cinnamon, optional
1 tablespoon honey, optional

1. Wash the quinoa, millet, and brown rice and rinse well.

2. Place the grains, water, and salt in a slow cooker. Cook on Low until most of the water has been absorbed, about 3 hours.

3. Add dried fruit and any optional ingredients and cook for 30 minutes more. If the mixture is too thick, add a little more water.

4. Serve hot or cold.

Serving suggestion:

Add a little nondairy milk of your choice to each bowl of cereal before serving.

Non Pantry Staple Grocery List
⅓ cup quinoa
⅓ cup millet
⅓ cup brown rice
½ cup dried raisins or cranberries
¼ cup chopped nuts of your choice
1 teaspoon vanilla extract

Calories 232
Fat 6 g
Saturated Fat 0.5 g
Cholesterol 0 mg
Sodium 105 mg
Total Carbs 42 g
Fiber 4 g
Protein 5 g

Nutty Goodness Granola

Hope Comerford
Clinton Township, MI

Makes about 10 cups

Prep. Time: 20 minutes ⚬ *Cooking Time: 4–6 hours* ⚬ *Ideal slow-cooker size: 6- to 7-qt.*

6 cups old-fashioned oats

¾ cup chopped almonds

½ cup chopped pecans

¾ cup raw sunflower seeds

¼ cup flaxseed

2 cups dried fruit

1 cup apple butter
(see recipe on pg. 35)

¼ cup honey

1. Place all of the dry ingredients in a bowl and stir.

2. Mix the apple butter and honey.

3. Spray your crock with a nonstick spray.

4. Pour your granola mixture in the crock with the apple butter mixture on top. Mix thoroughly.

5. Cover and cook on Low with the lid vented for 4 to 6 hours, stirring frequently (every 30 to 40 minutes) or until the granola is lightly browned and slightly clumpy.

Non Pantry Staple Grocery List
6 cups old-fashioned oats
¾ cup chopped almonds
½ cup chopped pecans
¾ cup raw sunflower seeds
¼ cup flaxseed
2 cups dried fruit
1 cup apple butter (see recipe on pg. 35)

Calories 305
Fat 8 g
Saturated Fat 1 g
Cholesterol 0 mg
Sodium 9 mg
Total Carbs 53 g
Fiber 5 g
Protein 7 g

Non Pantry Staple Grocery List
12 ounces soybeans, roasted with no salt
4 cups rolled oats
¾ cup soy flour
¾ cup ground flaxseed
1⅓ cups coarsely chopped nuts
¾ cup unsweetened applesauce
2 teaspoons vanilla extract

Soy-Flax Granola

Phyllis Good
Lancaster, PA

Makes 15 servings
Prep. Time: 20 minutes ❧ *Cooking Time: 2–3 hours* ❧ *Chilling Time: 2 hours* ❧ *Ideal slow-cooker size: 6-qt.*

12 ounces soybeans, roasted with no salt

4 cups gluten-free rolled oats

¾ cup soy flour

¾ cup ground flaxseeds

1 teaspoon salt

2 teaspoons cinnamon

1⅓ cups coarsely chopped nuts

¾ cup honey

½ cup coconut oil, melted

¾ cup unsweetened applesauce

2 teaspoons vanilla extract

Optional additions: dried cranberries, dried cherries, chopped dried apricots, chopped dried figs, raisins, or some combination of these dried fruits

Calories 459
Fat 25 g
Saturated Fat 25 g
Cholesterol 0 mg
Sodium 132 mg
Total Carbs 45 g
Fiber 9 g
Protein 19 g

1. Grease interior of slow-cooker crock.

2. Briefly process soybeans in a blender or food processor until coarsely chopped. Place in large bowl.

3. Add oats, flour, flaxseeds, salt, cinnamon, and nuts. Mix thoroughly with spoon.

4. In a smaller bowl, combine honey, coconut oil, unsweetened applesauce, and vanilla well.

5. Pour wet ingredients over dry. Stir well, remembering to stir up from the bottom, using either a strong spoon or your clean hands.

6. Pour mixture into crock. Cover, but vent the lid by propping it open with a chopstick or wooden spoon handle. Or if you're using an oval cooker, turn the lid sideways.

7. Cook on High for 1 hour, stirring up from the bottom and around the sides every 20 minutes or so. (Set a timer so you don't forget!)

8. Switch the cooker to Low. Bake for another 1 to 2 hours, still stirring every 20 minutes.

9. Granola is done when it eventually browns a bit and looks dry.

10. Pour granola onto parchment or a large baking sheet to cool and crisp up more.

11. Stir in any of the dried fruits that you want.

12. If you like clumps, no need to stir granola again while it cools. Otherwise, break up the granola with a spoon or your hands as it cools.

13. When completely cooled, store in airtight container.

Breakfast Apples

Joyce Bowman, Lady Lake, FL
Jeanette Oberholtzer, Manheim, PA

Makes 4 servings
Prep. Time: 10–15 minutes ⚬ *Cooking Time: 2–8 hours* ⚬ *Ideal slow-cooker size: 3-qt.*

4 medium apples, peeled and sliced

¼ cup honey

1 teaspoon cinnamon

2 tablespoons melted coconut oil

2 cups dry granola (see recipes on pgs. 29 and 31)

1. Place apples in your slow cooker.

2. Combine remaining ingredients. Sprinkle the mixture evenly over the apples.

3. Cover and cook on Low for 6 to 8 hours, or overnight, or on High for 2 to 3 hours.

Non Pantry Staple Grocery List

4 medium-sized apples

2 cups granola (see recipes on pgs. 29 and 31)

Calories 511

Fat 32 g

Saturated Fat 12 g

Cholesterol 0 mg

Sodium 7 mg

Total Carbs 57 g

Fiber 9 g

Protein 6 g

Apple Butter

Hope Comerford
Clinton Township, MI

Makes 6 cups
Prep. Time: 15 minutes ⚶ Cooking Time: 60 minutes ⚶ Setting: Manual
Pressure: High ⚶ Release: Natural

5 lb. apples, peeled, cored, and sliced

½ cup honey

¼ teaspoon ground cloves

½ teaspoon ground nutmeg

1 tablespoon cinnamon

Pinch salt

2 tablespoons lemon juice

1 tablespoon vanilla extract

1 cup water

1. Combine all of the ingredients in the inner pot of the Instant Pot and mix well.

2. Lock the lid in place; turn the vent to sealing.

3. Press Manual and set to 60 minutes on High.

4. When cooking time is over, let the steam release naturally.

5. Using an immersion blender, blend the apples until smooth.

TIP

This should keep in the refrigerator for up to 3 weeks in a tightly sealed container, or freeze extra in smaller serving sizes.

Non Pantry Staple Grocery List
5 lb. apples
2 tablespoons lemon juice
1 tablespoon vanilla extract

Calories 18
Fat 0 g
Saturated Fat 0 g
Cholesterol 0 mg
Sodium 3 mg
Total Carbs 5 g
Fiber 0 g
Protein 0 g

Pear Honey Butter

Becky Fixel
Grosse Pointe Farms, MI

Makes 45–50 servings
Prep. Time: 30 ⚜ Cooking Time: 10 hours ⚜ Ideal slow-cooker size: 6½- or 7-qt.

10 lb. ripened pears, peeled, cored, sliced

1 cup water

1 cup honey

1. Place your pear slices inside your slow cooker.

2. Add the water and honey.

3. Cover and cook on Low for 10 hours. You can stir if you want to, but it's not necessary. When your pears are done, they will have darkened in color, but won't dry out through cooking.

4. Either use your blender and puree your softened pears in batches until done or use an immersion blender to make a smooth consistency.

Non Pantry Staple Grocery List
10 lb. pears

Calories 37
Fat 1 g
Saturated Fat 0 g
Cholesterol 0 mg
Sodium 1 mg
Total Carbs 10 g
Fiber 1 g
Protein 0.5 g

Best Steel-Cut Oats

Colleen Heatwole
Burton, MI

Makes 4 servings

Prep. Time: 5 minutes · *Cooking Time: 3 minutes* · *Setting: Manual*
Pressure: High · *Release: Natural*

- 1 cup steel-cut oats
- 2 cups water
- 1 cup nondairy milk
- Pinch salt
- ½ teaspoon vanilla extract
- 1 cinnamon stick
- ¼ cup raisins
- ¼ cup dried cherries
- 1 teaspoon ground cinnamon
- ¼ cup toasted almonds
- Honey, optional

1. Add all ingredients to the inner pot of the Instant Pot except the toasted almonds and honey.

2. Secure the lid and make sure the vent is turned to sealing. Cook for 3 minutes on High, using the manual function.

3. Let the pressure release naturally.

4. Remove cinnamon stick.

5. Add almonds, and sweetener if desired, and serve.

Non Pantry Staple Grocery List

- 1 cup steel-cut oats
- 1 cup nondairy milk
- ½ teaspoon vanilla extract
- 1 cinnamon stick
- ¼ cup raisins
- ¼ cup dried cherries
- ¼ cup toasted almonds

Calories 276
Fat 7 g
Saturated Fat 1 g
Cholesterol 0 mg
Sodium 53 mg
Total Carbs 46 g
Fiber 7 g
Protein 9 g

Soups, Stews, and Chilies

Butternut Squash Soup

Colleen Heatwole
Burton, MI

Makes 4 servings

Prep. Time: 30 minutes ☙ *Cooking Time: 15 minutes* ☙ *Setting: Sauté and Manual*
Pressure: High ☙ *Release: Manual*

2 tablespoons olive oil

1 large onion, chopped

2 cloves minced garlic

1 teaspoon thyme

½ teaspoon sage

Salt and pepper to taste

2 large butternut squash, peeled, seeded, and cubed (about 4 lb.)

4 cups vegetable stock

1. In the inner pot of the Instant Pot, add the olive oil and set to the sauté function.

2. Add onion and garlic and cook until soft, 3 to 5 minutes.

3. Add thyme and sage and cook another minute. Season with salt and pepper.

4. Stir in butternut squash and add vegetable stock.

5. Secure the lid and make sure vent is at sealing. Using manual setting, cook squash and seasonings 10 minutes, using high pressure.

6. When time is up, do a quick release of the pressure.

7. Puree the soup in a food processor or use immersion blender right in the inner pot. If soup is too thick, add more stock. Adjust salt and pepper seasoning as needed.

Non Pantry Staple Grocery List
2 large butternut squash

Calories 288
Fat 8 g
Saturated Fat 1 g
Cholesterol 2 mg
Sodium 78 mg
Total Carbs 56 g
Fiber 9 g
Protein 6 g

Velvety Butternut Squash Soup

Carol Collins
Holly Springs, NC

Makes 4 servings
Prep. Time: 15 minutes ⚜ Cooking Time: 2–3 hours ⚜ Ideal slow-cooker size: 5-qt.

2 tablespoons minced shallot (or onion)

2 tablespoons olive oil

5 cups peeled, cubed butternut squash

2 cups peeled, cubed russet potatoes

4 cups vegetable broth

⅛ teaspoon cayenne pepper

1. In a small frying pan, sauté shallot or onion in olive oil until softened, about 5 minutes.

2. Place in slow cooker. Add squash, potatoes, vegetable broth, and cayenne pepper.

3. Cover. Cook on High for 2 to 3 hours, until potato and squash are very tender.

4. Use an immersible or stand blender to puree until smooth. Serve.

Non Pantry Staple Grocery List
2 tablespoons minced shallot
5 cups cubed butternut squash
2 cups cubed russet potatoes

Calories 239
Fat 7 g
Saturated Fat 1 g
Cholesterol 0 mg
Sodium 81 mg
Total Carbs 43 g
Fiber 6 g
Protein 4 g

Squash and Tomato Soup

Jean Harris Robinson
Pemberton, NJ

Makes 12 servings
Prep. Time: 25 minutes 🍃 Cooking Time: 4 hours 🍃 Ideal slow-cooker size: 5-qt.

2 tablespoons olive oil

2–3 whole garlic cloves

1 large onion, diced

5 carrots, diced

3 ribs celery, diced

2 lb. winter squash, peeled and cut into chunks

2 (14½-oz.) cans diced tomatoes

8 cups vegetable stock

½ cup chopped fresh basil leaves

½ cup chopped fresh cilantro leaves

2 tablespoons balsamic vinegar or rice vinegar

Salt and pepper to taste

1. Combine olive oil, garlic, onion, carrots, celery, squash, tomatoes, and stock in slow cooker.

2. Cover. Cook on Low for 4 hours or until vegetables are tender.

3. Add basil, cilantro, vinegar, and salt and pepper. Puree with hand blender or in stand blender.

Non Pantry Staple Grocery List

5 carrots

3 ribs celery

2 lb. winter squash

2 (14½-oz.) cans diced tomatoes

Bunch fresh basil

Bunch fresh cilantro

2 tablespoons balsamic or rice vinegar

Calories 98
Fat 2 g
Saturated Fat 0 g
Cholesterol 0 mg
Sodium 184 mg
Total Carbs 19 g
Fiber 3 g
Protein 2 g

Sweet Potato and Ginger Soup

Jenny Kempf
Bedminster, PA

Makes 4 servings
Prep. Time: 15 minutes ⚭ Cooking Time: 7–8 hours ⚭ Ideal slow-cooker size: 6-qt.

1 lb. sweet potatoes, peeled and cubed

2 teaspoons olive oil

2 teaspoons chopped garlic

2 teaspoons peeled, chopped ginger

2 cups vegetable stock

1 cup coconut milk

Salt and pepper to taste

2 tablespoons fresh chopped cilantro

3 scallions, chopped

Cashews, chopped, for garnish

1. Place sweet potatoes in slow cooker with olive oil, garlic, ginger, vegetable stock, coconut milk, salt, and pepper.

2. Cover and cook on Low for 7–8 hours, or until potatoes are tender.

3. Add cilantro and scallions.

4. Puree soup with hand blender or in stand blender. Pour into bowls or serving pot.

5. Sprinkle with cashews and serve.

Non Pantry Staple Grocery List
1 lb. sweet potatoes
2 teaspoons chopped fresh ginger
1 cup coconut milk
2 tablespoons fresh chopped cilantro
3 scallions
Cashews for garnish

Calories 220
Fat 11 g
Saturated Fat 8 g
Cholesterol 0 mg
Sodium 116 mg
Total Carbs 28 g
Fiber 4 g
Protein 3 g

Potato Soup

Janie Steele
Moore, OK

Makes 6 servings
Prep. Time: 20–30 minutes ❧ Cooking Time: 5–6 hours ❧ Ideal slow-cooker size: 4- to 6-qt.

6–8 cups vegetable broth

1 large onion, chopped

3 ribs celery, chopped, including leaves, if you like

6 large white potatoes, peeled, chopped, cubed, or sliced

Salt and pepper to taste

Optional ingredients:

Reduced-fat shredded sharp cheddar cheese

2–3 cups chopped clams

1 (10- or 16-oz.) package frozen corn

1. Place all ingredients in slow cooker.

2. Cover and cook on High for 5 hours or on Low for 6 hours, or until vegetables are soft but not mushy.

TIP

This recipe is vegetarian as written, but if that's not a concern, you can use chicken broth instead of vegetable broth.

Non Pantry Staple Grocery List
3 ribs celery
6 large white potatoes

Calories 279
Fat 5 g
Saturated Fat 2 g
Cholesterol 39 mg
Sodium 1162 mg
Total Carbs 39 g
Fiber 3 g
Protein 20 g

Potato Leek Soup

Melissa Paskvan
Novi, MI

Makes 4–6 servings
Prep. Time: 20 minutes   Cooking Time: 6 hours   Ideal slow-cooker size: 6-qt.

5 medium Yukon Gold potatoes, chopped

2 cups vegetable stock

2 cups water

2–3 bay leaves

½ head of cauliflower, broken up

3 ribs celery, whole

¼ teaspoon pepper

Salt to taste

3 large leeks, chopped (rinse leek well and include the tough tops)

1. Place all of the ingredients in the slow cooker and put the tough tops of the leeks on the top.

2. Cover and cook on Low for 6 hours.

3. Remove tough leek tops, celery, and bay leaves. Either blend all the ingredients in a blender or use an immersion blender while in the slow cooker and blend until very creamy. Salt to taste and add water if too thick for your liking.

Non Pantry Staple Grocery List
3 large leeks
5 medium Yukon Gold potatoes
½ head cauliflower
3 ribs celery

Calories 113
Fat 0 g
Saturated Fat 0 g
Cholesterol 0 mg
Sodium 64 mg
Total Carbs 30 g
Fiber 4 g
Protein 4 g

Slow-Cooker Tomato Soup

Becky Fixel
Grosse Pointe Farms, MI

Makes 8 servings
Prep. Time: 15 minutes ❧ *Cooking Time: 6 hours* ❧ *Ideal slow-cooker size: 6-qt.*

6–8 cups chopped fresh tomatoes

1 medium onion, chopped

2 teaspoons minced garlic

1 teaspoon basil

½ teaspoon pepper

½ teaspoon sea salt

½ teaspoon red pepper flakes

2 tablespoons chicken or vegetable bouillon

1 cup water

¾ cup fat-free half-and-half

1. Combine your tomatoes, onion, spices, bouillon, and 1 cup of water in your slow cooker.

2. Cover and cook on Low for 6 hours.

3. Add ¾ cup fat-free half-and-half and combine all ingredients with an immersion blender. Serve hot.

Non Pantry Staple Grocery List
6–8 cups chopped fresh tomatoes
2 tablespoons vegetable bouillon

Calories 72
Fat 3 g
Saturated Fat 2 g
Cholesterol 8 mg
Sodium 972 mg
Total Carbs 10 g
Fiber 2 g
Protein 3 g

Enchilada Soup

Melissa Paskvan
Novi, MI

Makes 6–8 servings
Prep. Time: 5 minutes   ❧   *Cooking Time: 6–8 hours*   ❧   *Ideal slow-cooker size: 6-qt.*

1 (14½-oz.) can of diced tomatoes with green chilies or chipotles

1 (12-oz.) jar enchilada sauce

4 cups vegetable broth

1 small onion, chopped

3 cups sliced tricolor peppers

1 (10-oz.) package frozen corn

1 cup water

½ cup uncooked quinoa

1. Add all ingredients to slow cooker.

2. Cover and cook on Low for 6 to 8 hours.

Non Pantry Staple Grocery List
1 (14½-oz.) can diced tomatoes with green chilies or chipotles
1 (12-oz.) jar enchilada sauce
3 cups sliced tricolor peppers
1 (10-oz.) package frozen corn
½ cup quinoa

Calories 132
Fat 2 g
Saturated Fat 1 g
Cholesterol 0 mg
Sodium 425 mg
Total Carbs 25 g
Fiber 3 g
Protein 4 g

Unstuffed Cabbage Soup

Colleen Heatwole
Burton, MI

Makes 4–6 servings
Prep. Time: 15 minutes ⚜ Cooking Time: 20 minutes ⚜ Setting: Manual
Pressure: High ⚜ Release: Natural then Manual

2 tablespoons olive oil

1 lb. ground turkey or meatless crumbles

1 medium onion, diced

2 garlic cloves, minced

1 small head cabbage, chopped, cored, cut into roughly 2-inch pieces.

1 (6-oz.) container tomato paste

1 (32-oz.) can diced tomatoes, with liquid

2 cups vegetable broth

1½ cups water

¾ cup brown rice

1–2 teaspoons salt to taste

½ teaspoon black pepper

1 teaspoon oregano

1 teaspoon parsley

1. Heat the olive oil in the inner pot of the Instant Pot using sauté function. Add ground turkey or crumbles. Stir frequently for about 2 minutes.

2. Add onion and garlic and continue to sauté for 2 more minutes, stirring frequently.

3. Add chopped cabbage.

4. On top of cabbage, layer tomato paste, tomatoes with liquid, vegetable broth, water, rice, and spices.

5. Secure the lid and set vent to "sealing." Using manual setting, select 20 minutes.

6. When time is up, let the pressure release naturally for 10 minutes, then do a quick release.

Non Pantry Staple Grocery List
1 lb. ground turkey or meatless crumbles
1 small head cabbage
1 (6-oz.) can tomato paste
1 (32-oz.) can diced tomatoes
¾ cup brown rice

Calories 28
Fat 6 g
Saturated Fat 1 g
Cholesterol 37 mg
Sodium 898 mg
Total Carbs 33 g
Fiber 3 g
Protein 23 g

Italian Bean Soup

Eylene Egan
Babylon, NY

Makes 8 servings
Prep. Time: 10 minutes ⚜ *Cooking Time: 8–10 hours* ⚜ *Ideal slow-cooker size: 4-qt.*

1 lb. dried baby lima beans

9 cups water

2 (8-oz.) cans low-sodium tomato sauce

3–4 cloves garlic, minced

6 cups water

Salt and pepper to taste

1. Place dried beans in large stockpot. Cover with 9 cups water. Cover pot and bring to a boil.

2. Boil for 10 minutes. Remove from heat and allow beans to stand for 1 hour, covered.

3. Return to stovetop, keep covered, and bring to a boil. Reduce heat to a simmer, and continue cooking for 2½ to 3 hours, or until beans are tender. Drain.

4. Place drained, cooked beans in slow cooker. Add remaining ingredients and stir together well.

5. Cover and cook on High for 1 hour, and then cook on Low for 4 to 5 hours.

Non Pantry Staple Grocery List
1 lb. dried baby lima beans
2 (8-oz.) cans low-sodium tomato sauce

Calories 205
Fat 1 g
Saturated Fat 0 g
Cholesterol 0 mg
Sodium 290 mg
Total Carbs 39 g
Fiber 13 g
Protein 12 g

Tofu and Vegetable Soup

Hope Comerford
Clinton Township, MI

Makes 4–6 servings
Prep. Time: 30 minutes ⚬ Cooking Time: 6–7 hours ⚬ Ideal slow-cooker size: 5-qt.

I lb. diced extra-firm tofu, drained and pressed

2 ribs celery, diced

I small yellow squash, diced

4 ounces sliced mushrooms

2 large carrots, diced

I medium onion, chopped

2 tablespoons garlic powder

I tablespoon onion powder

I tablespoon basil

½ teaspoon no-salt seasoning

I teaspoon salt

Black pepper to taste

32 ounces vegetable stock

1. Place the tofu, vegetables, and spices into the crock. Pour the vegetable stock over the top.

2. Cover and cook on Low for 6 to 7 hours, or until vegetables are tender.

Non Pantry Staple Grocery List
I lb. extra-firm tofu
2 ribs celery
I small yellow squash
4 ounces sliced mushrooms
2 large carrots

Calories 112
Fat 3 g
Saturated Fat 1 g
Cholesterol 0 mg
Sodium 400 mg
Total Carbs 13 g
Fiber 3 g
Protein 9 g

Vegetable Soup with Rice

Hope Comerford
Clinton Township, MI

Makes 6–8 servings
Prep. Time: 30 minutes ⚜ *Cooking Time: 6½–7½ hours* ⚜ *Ideal slow-cooker size: 3-qt.*

2 lb. extra-firm tofu, drained and pressed, then diced

1½ cups chopped carrots

1½ cups chopped red onion

2 tablespoons garlic powder

1 tablespoon onion powder

2 teaspoons kosher salt

¼ teaspoon celery seed

¼ teaspoon paprika

⅛ teaspoon pepper

1 dried bay leaf

8 cups vegetable stock

1 cup fresh green beans

3 cups cooked brown rice

1. Place tofu into the bottom of crock, then add rest of the remaining ingredients, except green beans and rice.

2. Cover and cook on Low for 6 to 7 hours.

3. Thirty minutes before you're ready to serve, add green beans. Cover and cook another 30 minutes.

4. To serve, place approximately ½ cup of the cooked rice into each bowl and ladle soup over the rice.

Non Pantry Staple Grocery List

2 lb. extra-firm tofu

1½ cups chopped carrots

1 cup fresh green beans

3 cups cooked brown rice

Calories 170

Fat 5 g

Saturated Fat 1 g

Cholesterol 0 mg

Sodium 578 mg

Total Carbs 16 g

Fiber 3 g

Protein 12 g

Hearty Bean and Vegetable Soup

Jewel Showalter
Landisville, PA

Makes 8–10 servings
Prep. Time: 20–25 minutes   ⚶   Cooking Time: 6–8 hours   ⚶   Ideal slow-cooker size: 5-qt.

2 medium onions, sliced
2 cloves garlic, minced
2 tablespoons olive oil
8 cups vegetable broth
1 small head cabbage, chopped
2 large red potatoes, chopped
2 cups chopped celery
2 cups chopped carrots
4 cups corn
2 teaspoons dried basil
1 teaspoon dried marjoram
¼ teaspoon dried oregano
1 teaspoon salt
½ teaspoon pepper
2 (15-oz.) cans navy beans, drained, rinsed

1. Sauté onions and garlic in oil in skillet. Transfer to large slow cooker.

2. Add remaining ingredients. Mix well.

3. Cover. Cook on Low for 6 to 8 hours.

Non Pantry Staple Grocery List
1 small head cabbage
2 large red potatoes
2 cups chopped celery
2 cups chopped carrots
4 cups corn
2 (15-oz.) cans navy beans

Calories 213
Fat 2 g
Saturated Fat 0 g
Cholesterol 0 mg
Sodium 187 mg
Total Carbs 42 g
Fiber 12 g
Protein 10 g

Black Bean Soup

Colleen Heatwole
Burton, MI

Makes 4–6 servings
Prep. Time: 20 minutes ⚶ *Cooking Time: 25 minutes unless beans soaked* ⚶ *Setting: Bean/Chili*
Pressure: High ⚶ *Release: Natural*

2 cups dry black beans, cleaned of debris and rinsed

6 cups vegetable stock

2 tablespoons olive oil

I cup coarsely chopped onion

3 cloves minced garlic

½ teaspoon paprika

⅛ teaspoon red pepper flakes

2 large bay leaves

I teaspoon cumin

2 teaspoons oregano

½ teaspoon salt, more if desired

Optional garnishes: yogurt, sour cream

1. Heat the oil in the inner pot of the Instant Pot with the sauté function. Add onion and sauté 2 minutes.

2. Add remaining ingredients, except garnishes, and stir well.

3. Secure lid and make sure vent is at sealing, then set to Bean/Chili for 25 minutes.

4. After time is up, let pressure release naturally.

5. Remove bay leaves and serve with desired garnishes.

Non Pantry Staple Grocery List
2 cups dry black beans

Calories 428
Fat 9 g
Saturated Fat 6 g
Cholesterol 3 mg
Sodium 335 mg
Total Carbs 63 g
Fiber 15 g
Protein 23 g

Ribollita

Orpha Herr
Andover, NY

Makes 6–8 servings
Prep. Time: 20 minutes   ♣   Standing Time: 8 hours or overnight   ♣   Cooking Time: 6–7 hours
Ideal slow-cooker size: 5-qt.

I cup dried white beans

3 tablespoons olive oil

¾ cup chopped onion

2 teaspoons minced garlic

I cup finely chopped celery

I cup finely chopped carrots

3 cups water, plus I cup more if needed

4 cups thinly sliced green cabbage

2 cups chopped tomatoes

I tablespoon dried parsley leaves

I teaspoon dried rosemary

I teaspoon dried oregano

½ teaspoon dried thyme leaves

⅛ teaspoon black pepper

I cup water, optional

2 teaspoons salt

Grated Parmesan cheese, for garnish, optional

1. In slow cooker, cover beans with 2 inches of water. Allow to soak overnight or 8 hours.

2. Drain.

3. Heat oil in a saucepan. Sauté onion, garlic, celery, and carrots.

4. Transfer sautéed vegetables to slow cooker with beans.

5. Add 3 cups water.

6. Cook on Low for 4 to 6 hours until beans are almost soft.

7. Add cabbage and tomatoes and parsley, rosemary, oregano, thyme, and pepper. Add another cup of water if needed. Cook on Low for another hour.

8. Add salt. Ladle into bowls.

9. Garnish with the optional grated Parmesan cheese and serve.

Non Pantry Staple Grocery List
I cup dried white beans
I cup finely chopped celery
I cup finely chopped carrots
4 cups thinly sliced green cabbage
2 cups chopped tomatoes
Grated Parmesan cheese

Calories 78
Fat 6 g
Saturated Fat 1 g
Cholesterol 0 mg
Sodium 512 mg
Total Carbs 7 g
Fiber 5 g
Protein 4 g

Tuscan Bean Soup

Jean Turner
Williams Lake, BC

Makes 4–6 servings
Prep. Time: 15 minutes ⚘ Cooking Time: 2 hours ⚘ Ideal slow-cooker size: 4-qt.

2 (14-oz.) cans diced tomatoes with herbs

1⅔ cups warm water

Salt and pepper to taste

2 cups Tuscan or curly kale, roughly shredded or chopped

1 (14-oz.) can cannellini beans or white beans, rinsed and drained

4 tablespoons extra-virgin olive oil

1. Combine tomatoes, warm water, salt, pepper, and kale in slow cooker.

2. Cook on High for 1 hour.

3. Add beans. Cook on High for another hour.

4. Place soup into bowls and drizzle each bowl with a little olive oil. Serve with warm crusty bread for dipping.

Non Pantry Staple Grocery List

2 (14-oz.) cans diced tomatoes with herbs

2 cups Tuscan or curly kale

1 (14-oz.) can cannellini beans or white beans

Calories 174
Fat 9 g
Saturated Fat 1 g
Cholesterol 0 mg
Sodium 294 mg
Total Carbs 18 g
Fiber 4 g
Protein 5 g

Chickpea Tortilla Soup

Hope Comerford
Clinton Township, MI

Makes 4–6 servings
Prep. Time: 5 minutes ⚶ Cooking Time: 6 hours ⚶ Ideal slow-cooker size: 4-qt.

2 (14½-oz.) cans petite diced tomatoes

2 (15-oz.) cans chickpeas, drained

6 cups vegetable stock

1 onion, chopped

1 (4-oz.) can diced green chilies

1 teaspoon chopped cilantro

3–4 fresh garlic cloves, minced

1 teaspoon sea salt

1 teaspoon pepper

1 teaspoon cumin

1 teaspoon paprika

1. Place all ingredients in slow cooker.

2. Cover and cook on Low for 6 hours.

Non Pantry Staple Grocery List
1 (14½-oz.) can petite diced
   tomatoes
1 (15-oz.) can chickpeas
1 (4-oz.) can diced green chilies
1 teaspoon chopped cilantro

Calories 66
Fat 4 g
Saturated Fat 0 g
Cholesterol 0 mg
Sodium 854 mg
Total Carbs 14 g
Fiber 10 g
Protein 12 g

Split Pea Soup

Judy Gascho
Woodburn, OR

Makes 3–4 servings
Prep. Time: 20 minutes ⚶ Cooking Time: 15 minutes ⚶ Setting: Manual
Pressure: High ⚶ Release: Manual

4 cups vegetable broth

4 sprigs thyme

2 tablespoons olive oil

2 ribs celery

2 carrots

I large leek

3 cloves garlic

12 ounces dried green split peas

Salt and pepper to taste

1. Pour the broth into the inner pot of the Instant Pot and set to sauté. Add the thyme and olive oil.

2. While the broth heats, chop the celery and cut the carrots into ½-inch-thick rounds, halve the leek lengthwise, and thinly slice and chop the garlic. Add the vegetables to the pot as you cut them. Rinse the split peas in a colander, discarding any small stones, then add to the pot.

3. Secure the lid, making sure the steam valve is in the sealing position. Set the cooker to High for 15 minutes. When the time is up, carefully turn the steam valve to the venting position to release the pressure manually.

4. Turn off the Instant Pot. Remove the lid and stir the soup; discard the thyme sprigs.

5. Thin the soup with up to 1 cup water if needed (the soup will continue to thicken as it cools). Season with salt and pepper.

Non Pantry Staple Grocery List
4 sprigs thyme
2 ribs celery
2 carrots
I large leek
12 ounces dried green split peas

Calories 130
Fat 4 g
Saturated Fat 1 g
Cholesterol 2 mg
Sodium 109 mg
Total Carbs 20 g
Fiber 2 g
Protein 6 g

Veggie Pea Soup

Diana Kampnich
Croghan, NY

Makes 6–8 servings
Prep. Time: 10 minutes ⚹ Cooking Time: 6 hours ⚹ Ideal slow-cooker size: 5-qt.

1 lb. (2 cups) dry split green peas
1 large onion, diced
2 ribs celery, diced
4 carrots, diced
2 medium potatoes, unpeeled, diced
8 cups water
2 teaspoons diced fresh garlic
1 teaspoon seasoned salt
1/8 teaspoon pepper
2 tablespoons apple cider vinegar, optional

1. Mix peas, onion, celery, carrots, potatoes, water, garlic, seasoned salt, and pepper in slow cooker.

2. Cover. Cook on Low for 6 hours. If you wish, add vinegar just before serving.

Non Pantry Staple Grocery List
1 lb. dry split green peas
2 ribs celery
4 carrots
2 medium potatoes
Apple cider vinegar

Calories 263
Fat 1 g
Saturated Fat 0 g
Cholesterol 0 mg
Sodium 242 mg
Total Carbs 47 g
Fiber 17 g
Protein 15 g

Brown Lentil Soup

Colleen Heatwole
Burton, MI

Makes 3–5 servings
Prep. Time: 15 minutes ⚬ *Cooking Time: 20 minutes* ⚬ *Setting: Sauté and Manual*
Pressure: High ⚬ *Release: Manual*

1 tablespoon olive oil
1 medium onion chopped, about 1 cup
1 medium carrot diced, about 1 cup
2 cloves garlic, minced
1 small bay leaf
1 lb. brown lentils
5 cups vegetable broth
1 teaspoon salt
¼ teaspoon ground black pepper
½ teaspoon lemon juice

1. Using the sauté function, sauté the onion in the inner pot of the Instant Pot with the olive oil for about 2 minutes, or until it starts to soften.

2. Add the carrot and sauté for 3 minutes more until it begins to soften. Stir frequently or it will stick.

3. Add the garlic and sauté for 1 more minute.

4. Add the bay leaf, lentils, and broth to pot.

5. Secure the lid and make sure vent is at sealing. Using manual setting, select 14 minutes and cook on High.

6. When cooking time is up, do a Quick Release of the pressure.

7. Discard bay leaf.

8. Stir in salt, pepper, and lemon juice, then adjust seasonings to taste.

Non Pantry Staple Grocery List
1 medium carrot
1 lb. brown lentils
½ teaspoon lemon juice

Calories 150
Fat 4 g
Saturated Fat 1 g
Cholesterol 2 mg
Sodium 78 mg
Total Carbs 5 g
Fiber 1 g
Protein 10 g

Red Lentil Soup

Barbara Landis
Lititz, PA

Makes 4 servings
Prep. Time: 10 minutes ♣ *Cooking Time: 4–8 hours* ♣ *Ideal slow-cooker size: 5-qt.*

6 cups vegetable broth

1 cup dry red lentils

3 carrots, sliced

1 medium onion, chopped

3 ribs celery, chopped

3 tablespoons uncooked brown rice

2 tablespoons minced garlic

1½ teaspoons herbes de Provence

½ teaspoon salt

¼ teaspoon pepper

1. Mix all ingredients in slow cooker.

2. Cover. Cook on Low for 7 to 8 hours, or on High for 4 to 5 hours.

Non Pantry Staple Grocery List
1 cup dry red lentils
3 carrots
3 ribs celery
3 tablespoons uncooked brown rice

Calories 460
Fat 3 g
Saturated Fat 0 g
Cholesterol 0 mg
Sodium 802 mg
Total Carbs 83 g
Fiber 18 g
Protein 25 g

Lentil Spinach Soup

Marilyn Widrick
Adams, NY

Makes 4–6 servings
Prep. Time: 10 minutes ⚹ *Cooking Time: 7½ hours* ⚹ *Ideal slow-cooker size: 5-qt.*

1 tablespoon olive oil

4 medium carrots, chopped

1 small onion, diced

1 teaspoon ground cumin

1 (14½-oz.) can diced tomatoes

1 (14½-oz.) can vegetable broth

1 cup dry lentils

2 cups water

¼ teaspoon salt

⅛ teaspoon pepper

1 (5-oz.) bag fresh spinach, chopped

1. Heat 1 tablespoon olive oil in cooking pot. Add carrots and onion. Cook for 8 to 10 minutes over medium heat.

2. Place in slow cooker. Add cumin, diced tomatoes, vegetable broth, dry lentils, water, salt, and pepper.

3. Cover and cook on Low for 7 hours.

4. Add spinach. Cook on Low for an additional 15 to 25 minutes.

Non Pantry Staple Grocery List
4 medium carrots
1 (14½-oz.) can diced tomatoes
1 cup dry lentils
1 (5-oz.) bag fresh spinach

Calories 311
Fat 4 g
Saturated Fat 0 g
Cholesterol 0 mg
Sodium 343 mg
Total Carbs 51 g
Fiber 13 g
Protein 17 g

Lentil Soup with Lemon

Heidi Wood
Vacaville, CA

Makes 6 servings
Prep. Time: 5 minutes   *Cooking Time: 7–8 hours*   *Ideal slow-cooker size: 5-qt.*

⅓ cup olive oil

2 large sweet onions, chopped

4 cloves garlic, minced

2 teaspoons ground cumin

½ teaspoon salt

½ teaspoon freshly ground black pepper

¼ teaspoon chili powder

8 cups water or vegetable broth

2 cups dry red lentils

2 large carrots, diced

2 tablespoons tomato paste

4 tablespoons lemon juice

1 cup chopped fresh cilantro

Plain yogurt, optional

1. Heat olive oil in a medium pan over medium-high heat. Stir in the onions and garlic, and cook until the onions are golden brown, about 5 minutes. Pour contents into the crock.

2. Place the remaining ingredients except the lemon juice, fresh cilantro, and optional yogurt into the crock and stir.

3. Cover and cook on Low for 7 to 8 hours.

4. Just before serving, stir lemon juice into the pot of soup.

5. Ladle soup into bowls. Serve cilantro on the side to be added as a garnish. It is also good with a dollop of plain yogurt for a slightly different taste.

Non Pantry Staple Grocery List

2 cups dry red lentils

2 large carrots

2 tablespoons tomato paste

4 tablespoons lemon juice

1 cup chopped fresh cilantro

Plain yogurt, optional

Calories 391
Fat 13 g
Saturated Fat 2 g
Cholesterol 0 mg
Sodium 678 mg
Total Carbs 55 g
Fiber 9 g
Protein 17 g

Tomato Lentil Soup

Elaine Sue Good
Tiskilwa, IL

Makes 8 servings
Prep. Time: 15 minutes ❧ Cooking Time: 6–10 hours ❧ Ideal slow-cooker size: 5-qt.

3 carrots, sliced

I onion, chopped

2 cloves garlic, minced

3 (15-oz.) cans diced tomatoes

2 cups vegetable broth

2 cups dry red lentils

⅓ cup chopped fresh basil

1. Combine carrots, onion, garlic, tomatoes, broth, and lentils in your slow cooker.

2. Cook on Low for 10 hours or on High for 6 hours, until lentils are tender.

3. An hour before cook time is up, add the fresh basil.

TIP

The amount of liquid needed for this recipe will vary depending on how hot your slow cooker heats. Check after 8 hours on Low or after 4 hours on High to be sure the soup isn't cooking dry.

Non Pantry Staple Grocery List

3 carrots

3 (15-oz.) cans diced tomatoes

2 cups dry red lentils

⅓ cup chopped fresh basil

Calories 228
Fat 0.5 g
Saturated Fat 0 g
Cholesterol 0 mg
Sodium 363 mg
Total Carbs 43 g
Fiber 7 g
Protein 13 g

Chipotle Navy Bean Soup

Rebecca Weybright
Manheim, PA

Makes 6 servings
Prep. Time: 10 minutes ❧ Cooking Time: 8 hours
Standing Time: 12 hours ❧ Ideal slow-cooker size: 5-qt.

1½ cups dried navy beans, soaked overnight

1 onion, chopped

1 dried chipotle chile, soaked for 10–15 minutes in cold water

4 cups water

1–2 teaspoons salt

2 cups canned tomatoes with juice

1. Drain soaked beans.

2. Add beans to slow cooker with the onion, chile, and water.

3. Cover and cook on Low for 8 hours until beans are creamy.

4. Add salt and tomatoes.

5. Use an immersion blender to puree soup.

Non Pantry Staple Grocery List
1½ cups dried navy beans
1 dried chipotle
2 cups canned tomatoes

Calories 196
Fat 1 g
Saturated Fat 0 g
Cholesterol 0 mg
Sodium 472 mg
Total Carbs 36 g
Fiber 8 g
Protein 12 g

"Meatball" and Pasta Soup

Michele Ruvola
Vestal, NY

Makes 4–5 servings
Prep. Time: 10 minutes   ⚜   Cooking Time: 9 minutes   ⚜   Setting: Manual
Pressure: High   ⚜   Release: Manual

I cup diced carrots

½ cup diced celery

¾ cup diced onion

I (12.7-oz.) bag frozen meatless meatballs

1½ cups whole wheat wide, flat pasta, such as pappardelle broken into shorter pieces

40 ounces vegetable broth

I teaspoon salt

½ teaspoon black pepper

2 tablespoons diced parsley

2 tablespoons diced scallions

1. Place all ingredients, except the parsley and scallions, in the inner pot of the Instant Pot and stir.

2. Secure the lid, make sure vent is set to sealing, then put on Manual function, set to high pressure, for 9 minutes.

3. Use quick release to release pressure, then stir.

4. Top with parsley and scallions.

Non Pantry Staple Grocery List

I cup diced carrots

½ cup diced celery

I (12.7-oz.) bag frozen meatless meatballs

1½ cups whole wheat ditalini pasta

2 tablespoons diced parsley

Calories 304
Fat 7 g
Saturated Fat 1 g
Cholesterol 0 mg
Sodium 1126 mg
Total Carbs 41 g
Fiber 8 g
Protein 21 g

Pumpkin and Chickpea Stew

Andrea Maher
Dunedin, FL

Makes 6 servings
Prep. Time: 10 minutes & Cooking Time: 3–8 hours & Ideal slow-cooker size: 5- or 6-qt.

3 cups canned pumpkin puree

4 cups canned chickpeas, drained

3 cups sliced mushrooms

1½ cups gluten-free low-sodium chicken broth

1½ cups plain nonfat Greek yogurt

Salt to taste

Pepper to taste

Red pepper and chili powder to taste, optional

1. Add all ingredients to slow cooker.

2. Cook on High for 3 to 4 hours or Low for 6 to 8 hours.

Non Pantry Staple Grocery List
3 cups canned pumpkin
4 cups canned chickpeas
3 cups sliced mushrooms
1½ cups plain nonfat Greek yogurt

Calories 316
Fat 5 g
Saturated Fat 1 g
Cholesterol 3 mg
Sodium 433 mg
Total Carbs 50 g
Fiber 15 g
Protein 21 g

Moroccan Spiced Stew

Melissa Paskvan
Novi, MI

Makes 6–8 servings
Prep. Time: 10 minutes ⚬ Cooking Time: 8 hours ⚬ Ideal slow-cooker size: 5-qt.

3 cups canned chopped tomatoes

3 cups vegetable stock

½ cup quinoa, rinsed

I can chickpeas, drained

I medium onion, chopped

⅛ teaspoon fresh zested ginger

1½ teaspoons cumin

¾ teaspoon cinnamon

¾ teaspoon turmeric

⅛–¼ teaspoon cayenne pepper

½ cup shredded or chopped carrots

3 cups chopped sweet potato

Salt and pepper to taste

1. Place all ingredients in the crock and mix well to incorporate the spices.

2. Cover and cook on Low for 8 hours.

Serving suggestion:

Top with harissa for a zesty warm flavor. Ladle this stew over brown rice or millet, and it is a filling meal. Cook with ½ cup dried apricots or dates to impart a sweet taste.

Non Pantry Staple Grocery List

3 cups canned chopped tomatoes

½ cup quinoa

I can chickpeas

⅛ teaspoon fresh zested ginger

½ cup shredded or chopped carrots

3 cups chopped sweet potato

Calories 196
Fat 2 g
Saturated Fat 0 g
Cholesterol 0 mg
Sodium 211 mg
Total Carbs 38 g
Fiber 7 g
Protein 7 g

White Chili

Rebecca Plank Leichty
Harrisonburg, VA

Makes 6–8 servings
Prep. Time: 15 minutes ⚘ *Cooking Time: 4–10 hours* ⚘ *Ideal slow-cooker size: 5-qt.*

1 (15-oz.) can chickpeas, drained, rinsed

1 (15-oz.) can navy beans, drained, rinsed

1 (15-oz.) can pinto beans, drained, rinsed

2 (1-lb.) bags frozen corn

2 tablespoons minced onions

1 red bell pepper, diced

3 teaspoons minced garlic

3 teaspoons ground cumin

½ teaspoon salt

½ teaspoon dried oregano

4 cups vegetable broth

1. Combine all ingredients in slow cooker.

2. Cover. Cook on Low for 8 to 10 hours or on High for 4 to 5 hours.

TIP
For more zip, add 2 teaspoons chili powder, or one or more chopped jalapeño peppers, to step 1.

Non Pantry Staple Grocery List
1 (15-oz.) can chickpeas
1 (15-oz.) can navy beans
1 (15-oz.) can pinto beans
2 (1-lb.) bags frozen corn
1 red bell pepper

Calories 326
Fat 3.5 g
Saturated Fat 1 g
Cholesterol 0 mg
Sodium 503 mg
Total Carbs 59 g
Fiber 15 g
Protein 19 g

White and Green Chili

Hope Comerford
Clinton Township, MI

Makes 6 servings
Prep. Time: 20 minutes ⚭ Cooking Time: 7–8 hours ⚭ Ideal slow-cooker size: 4-qt.

1 lb. meatless crumbles

1 cup chopped onion

2 (15-oz.) cans great northern beans, drained and rinsed

1 (16-oz.) jar salsa verde (green salsa)

2 cups vegetable stock

1 (4-oz.) can green chilies

1½ teaspoons ground cumin

1 teaspoon sea salt

¼ teaspoon black pepper

2 tablespoons fresh chopped cilantro

⅓ cup plain nonfat Greek yogurt, optional

1. Place all ingredients in crock except cilantro and Greek yogurt. Stir.

2. Cover and cook on Low for 7–8 hours. Stir in cilantro.

Non Pantry Staple Grocery List

1 lb. meatless crumbles

2 (15-oz.) cans great northern beans

1 (16 oz.) jar salsa verde

1 (4-oz.) can green chilies

2 tablespoons fresh chopped cilantro

⅓ cup plain nonfat Greek yogurt, optional

Calories 302
Fat 2 g
Saturated Fat 0 g
Cholesterol 0 mg
Sodium 1580 mg
Total Carbs 48 g
Fiber 13 g
Protein 31 g

Pumpkin Chili

Hope Comerford
Clinton Township, MI

Makes 8 servings
Prep. Time: 10 minutes ⚬ Cooking Time: 7–8 hours ⚬ Ideal slow-cooker size: 6-qt.

1 (16-oz.) can kidney beans, drained and rinsed

1 (16-oz.) can black beans, drained and rinsed

1 large onion, chopped

½ green pepper, chopped

1 lb. ground turkey or meatless crumbles

1 (15-oz.) can pumpkin puree

4 cups fresh chopped tomatoes

3 tablespoons garlic powder

1 tablespoon ancho chili powder

1 teaspoon salt

2 teaspoons cumin

¼ teaspoon pepper

5 cups vegetable stock

1. In your slow cooker, place the kidney beans, black beans, onion, and green pepper.

2. Crumble the ground turkey (or spread the meatless crumbles) over the top and spoon the pumpkin puree on top of that.

3. Add the remaining ingredients and stir.

4. Cover and cook on Low for 7 to 8 hours.

Non Pantry Staple Grocery List
1 (16-oz.) can kidney beans
1 (16-oz.) can black beans
½ green pepper
1 lb. ground turkey or meatless crumbles
4 cups fresh chopped tomatoes

Calories 276
Fat 2 g
Saturated Fat 0.5 g
Cholesterol 28 mg
Sodium 2274 mg
Total Carbs 42 g
Fiber 12 g
Protein 26 g

Black Bean Chili

Kenda Autumn
San Francisco, CA

Makes 6–8 servings
Prep. Time: 15 minutes ❧ Cooking Time: 8 hours ❧ Ideal slow-cooker size: 5-qt.

1 tablespoon olive oil
1 onion, chopped
1 teaspoon ground cumin
1 teaspoon ground coriander
1 tablespoon chili powder
1 teaspoon garam masala
1 (16-oz.) can black beans, rinsed and drained
1 (14-oz.) can diced tomatoes
1 sweet potato, cubed
1 cup corn

1. Heat olive oil in saucepan. Brown onion, cumin, coriander, chili powder, and garam masala.

2. Transfer sauté to slow cooker.

3. Add beans, tomatoes, sweet potato, and corn.

4. Cover and cook on Low for 8 hours.

Non Pantry Staple Grocery List
1 (16-oz.) can black beans
1 (14-oz.) can diced tomatoes
1 sweet potato
1 cup corn

Calories 143
Fat 3 g
Saturated Fat 0 g
Cholesterol 0 mg
Sodium 165 mg
Total Carbs 25 g
Fiber 7 g
Protein 7 g

"Beef" and Kale Stew

Dora Martindale
Elk City, OK

Makes 6 servings
Prep. Time: 20 minutes ❧ Cooking Time: 10 minutes ❧ Setting: Sauté and Manual
Pressure: High ❧ Release: Manual and Natural

3 tablespoons olive oil

2 lb. meatless crumbles

1 cup sliced mushrooms

4 pieces vegetarian "bacon," chopped

2 bundles kale, finely chopped

2 onions, chopped

4 cloves garlic

3 large potatoes, chopped

3–4 cups vegetable stock

2 tablespoons dried thyme

3 teaspoons salt (or more to taste)

1 teaspoon pepper (or more to taste)

2 (heaping) teaspoons cornstarch

1. In the inner pot of the Instant Pot, sauté mushrooms using in the olive oil using the sauté function, then place in a bowl.

2. Add the meatless crumbles, chopped "bacon," kale, onions, and garlic, and sauté using the sauté function until the kale is reduced in size.

3. Add the potatoes, vegetable stock, thyme, salt, and pepper. Secure the lid and make sure vent is at sealing, then cook on manual, high pressure for 8 minutes. Let the pressure release naturally.

4. Thicken slightly with the cornstarch and add more salt or pepper as needed.

NOTES

• I also make a version of this and use butternut squash or sweet potatoes in place of the potatoes.

• You can add just about any veggies to this.

Non Pantry Staple Grocery List

2 lb. meatless crumbles

4 pieces vegetarian "bacon"

2 bundles kale

1 cup sliced mushrooms

3 large potatoes

2 teaspoons cornstarch

Calories 997

Fat 48 g

Saturated Fat 7 g

Cholesterol 0 mg

Sodium 4663 mg

Total Carbs 69 g

Fiber 26 g

Protein 88 g

Main Dishes

Honey Lemon Garlic Salmon

Judy Gascho
Woodburn, OR

Makes
Prep. Time: 15 minutes ⚜ Cooking Time: 5–12 minutes ⚜ Setting: Manual
Pressure: High ⚜ Release: Manual

5 tablespoons olive oil

3 tablespoons honey

2–3 tablespoons lemon juice

3 cloves garlic, minced

4 (3–4-oz.) fresh salmon fillets

Salt and pepper to taste

1–2 tablespoons minced parsley (dried or fresh)

Lemon slices, optional

Non Pantry Staple Grocery List
4 (3–4 oz.) fresh salmon fillets
2–3 tablespoons lemon juice
1–2 tablespoons fresh or dried parsley
1 lemon, optional

Calories 352
Fat 22 g
Saturated Fat 4 g
Cholesterol 57 mg
Sodium 81 mg
Total Carbs 15 g
Fiber 0 g
Protein 26 g

1. Mix olive oil, honey, lemon juice, and minced garlic in a bowl.

2. Place each salmon fillet on a piece of foil big enough to wrap up the piece of fish.

3. Brush each fillet generously with the olive oil mixture.

4. Sprinkle with salt, pepper, and parsley flakes.

5. Top each with a thin slice of lemon if desired.

6. Wrap each fillet and seal well at top.

7. Place 1½ cups of water in the inner pot of your Instant Pot and place the trivet in the pot.

8. Place wrapped fillets on the trivet.

9. Close the lid and turn valve to sealing.

10. Cook on manual at high pressure for 5 to 8 minutes for smaller pieces, or for 10 to 12 minutes if they are large.

11. Carefully release pressure at the end of the cooking time manually.

12. Unwrap and enjoy.

Lemon Dijon Fish

June S. Groff
Denver, PA

Makes 4 servings
Prep. Time: 10 minutes ⚶ Cooking Time: 3 hours ⚶ Ideal slow-cooker size: 2-qt.

1½ lb. orange roughy fillets
2 tablespoons Dijon mustard
3 tablespoons olive oil, melted
1 teaspoon Worcestershire sauce
1 tablespoon lemon juice

1. Cut fillets to fit in slow cooker.

2. In a bowl, mix remaining ingredients. Pour sauce over fish. (If you have to stack the fish, spoon a portion of the sauce over the first layer of fish before adding the second layer.)

3. Cover and cook on Low for 3 hours, or until fish flakes easily but is not dry or overcooked.

Non Pantry Staple Grocery List
1½ lb. orange roughy fillets
2 tablespoons Dijon mustard
1 teaspoon Worcestershire sauce
1 tablespoon lemon juice

Calories 320
Fat 20 g
Saturated Fat 3 g
Cholesterol 102 mg
Sodium 273 mg
Total Carbs 1 g
Fiber 0 g
Protein 32 g

Spiced Cod

Hope Comerford
Clinton Township, MI

Makes 4–6 servings
Prep. Time: 8 minutes   ⚇   Cooking Time: 2 hours   ⚇   Ideal slow-cooker size: 4- or 5-qt.

4–6 cod fillets
½ cup thinly sliced red onion
1½ teaspoons garlic powder
1½ teaspoons onion powder
½ teaspoon cumin
¼ teaspoon ancho chili powder
Juice of 1 lime
⅓ cup vegetable broth

1. Place fish in the crock. Place the onion on top.

2. Mix the remaining ingredients and pour over the fish.

3. Cover and cook on Low for 2 hours, or until fish flakes easily with a fork.

Serving suggestion:

Serve on a bed of quinoa or brown rice with Lemony Garlic Asparagus.

Non Pantry Staple Grocery List
4–6 cod fillets
1 lime

Calories 201
Fat 2 g
Saturated Fat 0 g
Cholesterol 9 mg
Sodium 146 mg
Total Carbs 3 g
Fiber 0.5 g
Protein 42 g

Cajun Catfish

Hope Comerford
Clinton Township, MI

Makes 4 servings
Prep. Time: 5 minutes ✤ *Cooking Time: 2 hours* ✤ *Ideal slow-cooker size: 6-qt.*

4 (6-oz.) catfish fillets
2 teaspoons paprika
1 teaspoon black pepper
1 teaspoon oregano
1 teaspoon dried thyme
½ teaspoon garlic powder
½ teaspoon kosher salt
½ teaspoon parsley flakes
¼ teaspoon cayenne pepper
1 tablespoon olive oil

1. Pat the catfish fillets dry.

2. Mix the paprika, black pepper, oregano, thyme, garlic powder, salt, parsley flakes, and cayenne.

3. Place parchment paper in your crock and push it down, so it forms against the inside of the crock. Place the olive oil in the crock.

4. Coat each side of the catfish fillets with the spice mixture, then place them in the crock.

5. Cover and cook on Low for about 2 hours, or until the fish flakes easily with a fork.

Non Pantry Staple Grocery List
4 (6-oz.) catfish fillets

Calories 240
Fat 14 g
Saturated Fat 3 g
Cholesterol 94 mg
Sodium 288 mg
Total Carbs 2 g
Fiber 1 g
Protein 26 g

Herbed Flounder

Dorothy VanDeest
Memphis, TX

Makes 6 servings
Prep. Time: 10 minutes   *Cooking Time: 2–3 hours*   *Ideal slow-cooker size: 6-qt.*

2 lb. flounder fillets, fresh or frozen

¾ cup vegetable stock

2 tablespoons lemon juice

2 tablespoons dried chives

2 tablespoons dried minced onion

½–1 teaspoon leaf marjoram

4 tablespoons chopped fresh parsley

½ teaspoon sea salt

1. Wipe fish as dry as possible. Cut fish into portions to fit slow cooker.

2. Combine stock and lemon juice. Stir in remaining ingredients except for the salt.

3. Sprinkle with salt.

4. Cover and cook on High for 2 to 3 hours, or until fish is flaky.

Non Pantry Staple Grocery List
2 lb. flounder fillets (fresh or frozen)
2 tablespoons lemon juice
4 tablespoons chopped fresh parsley

Calories 130
Fat 3 g
Saturated Fat 1 g
Cholesterol 73 mg
Sodium 279 mg
Total Carbs 1 g
Fiber 0 g
Protein 25 g

Herby Chicken

Joyce Bowman
Lady Lake, FL

Makes 4–6 servings
Prep. Time: 10 minutes ♣ Cooking Time: 5–7 hours ♣ Ideal slow-cooker size: 5-qt.

2½–3½-lb. whole roaster chicken

1 lemon, cut into wedges

1 bay leaf

2–4 sprigs fresh thyme, or ¾ teaspoon dried thyme

Salt and pepper to taste

1. Remove giblets from chicken.

2. Put lemon wedges and bay leaf in cavity.

3. Place whole chicken in slow cooker.

4. Scatter sprigs of thyme over the chicken. Sprinkle with salt and pepper.

5. Cover and cook on Low for 5 to 7 hours, or until chicken is tender.

6. Serve hot with whole wheat pasta or brown rice, or debone and freeze for your favorite casseroles or salads.

Non Pantry Staple Grocery List
2½–3½-lb. whole roaster chicken
1 lemon
2–4 sprigs fresh thyme (or
   ¾ teaspoon dried thyme)

Calories 460
Fat 31 g
Saturated Fat 9 g
Cholesterol 226 mg
Sodium 159 mg
Total Carbs 2 g
Fiber 1 g
Protein 44 g

Italian Slow-Cooker Chicken

Andrea Maher
Dunedin, FL

Makes 6 servings

Prep. Time: 5 minutes ⚜ Cooking Time: 3–8 hours ⚜ Ideal slow-cooker size: 6-qt.

24 ounces boneless, skinless chicken breast, cut into small pieces

3 cups canned chickpeas

16 ounces frozen spinach

2 cups sliced mushrooms, zucchini, chopped tomatoes, or other favorite vegetables (or a mix)

2 tablespoons Italian seasoning

1 cup vegetable stock

1. Add all ingredients to the slow cooker.

2. Cover and cook on Low for 6 to 8 hours or High for 3 to 4 hours.

Serving suggestion:

Serve over couscous. Garnish with fresh parsley or cilantro.

Non Pantry Staple Grocery List

24 ounces boneless, skinless chicken breast

3 cups canned chickpeas

16 ounces frozen spinach

2 cups sliced mushrooms, zucchini, chopped tomatoes, or other favorite vegetables (or a mix)

Calories 304
Fat 6 g
Saturated Fat 1 g
Cholesterol 83 mg
Sodium 128 mg
Total Carbs 29 g
Fiber 9 g
Protein 36 g

Garlic Galore Rotisserie Chicken

Hope Comerford
Clinton Township, MI

Makes 4 servings
Prep. Time: 5 minutes ♳ *Cooking Time: 33 minutes* ♳ *Setting: Sauté and Manual*
Pressure: High ♳ *Release: Natural Release then Manual*

3-lb. whole chicken, innards removed

2 tablespoons olive oil, divided

Salt to taste

Pepper to taste

20–30 cloves fresh garlic, peeled and left whole

1 cup vegetable broth

2 tablespoons garlic powder

2 teaspoons onion powder

½ teaspoon basil

½ teaspoon cumin

½ teaspoon chili powder

Non Pantry Staple Grocery List
3-lb. whole chicken

Calories 333
Fat 23 g
Saturated Fat 5 g
Cholesterol 114 mg
Sodium 110 mg
Total Carbs 9 g
Fiber 1 g
Protein 24 g

1. Rub chicken with one tablespoon of the olive oil and sprinkle with salt and pepper.

2. Place the garlic cloves inside the chicken. Use butcher's twine to secure the legs.

3. Press the sauté button on the Instant Pot, then add the rest of the olive oil to the inner pot.

4. When the pot is hot, place the chicken inside. You are just trying to sear it, so leave it for about 4 minutes on each side.

5. Remove the chicken and set aside. Place the trivet at the bottom of the inner pot and pour in the vegetable broth.

6. Mix the remaining seasonings and rub the mixture all over the entire chicken.

7. Place the chicken back inside the inner pot, breast-side up, on top of the trivet and secure the lid to the sealing position.

8. Press the Manual button and use the +/- to set it for 25 minutes.

9. When the timer beeps, allow the pressure to release naturally for 15 minutes. If the lid will not open at this point, quick release the remaining pressure and remove the chicken.

10. Let the chicken rest for 5 to 10 minutes before serving.

Garlic and Lemon Chicken

Hope Comerford
Clinton Township, MI

Makes 4–6 servings
Prep. Time: 5 minutes ⚬ *Cooking Time: 5–6 hours* ⚬ *Ideal slow-cooker size: 3- to 5-qt.*

4–5 lb. boneless, skinless chicken breasts or thighs

½ cup minced shallot

½ cup olive oil

¼ cup lemon juice

I tablespoon garlic paste (or use I large clove garlic, minced)

I tablespoon no-salt seasoning

⅛ teaspoon pepper

1. Place chicken in slow cooker.

2. In a small bowl, mix the remaining ingredients. Pour this mixture over the chicken in the crock.

3. Cover and cook on Low for 5 to 6 hours.

Non Pantry Staple Grocery List
4–5 lb. boneless, skinless chicken breasts or thighs
½ cup minced shallot
¼ cup lemon juice
I tablespoon garlic paste

Calories 641
Fat 31 g
Saturated Fat 5 g
Cholesterol 264 mg
Sodium 165 mg
Total Carbs 4 g
Fiber 0.5 g
Protein 82 g

Lemon and Olive Oil Chicken

Judy Gascho
Woodburn, OR

Makes 4 servings
Prep. Time: 15 minutes ⚸ Cooking Time: 7 minutes ⚸ Setting: Poultry
Pressure: High ⚸ Release: Natural

2 tablespoons olive oil

1 medium onion, chopped

4 cloves garlic, minced

½ teaspoon paprika

1 tablespoon chopped fresh parsley, or
1 teaspoon dried parsley

½ teaspoon pepper

2 lb. boneless chicken breasts or thighs

⅔ cup vegetable broth

⅓ cup lemon juice

1 teaspoon salt

1–2 tablespoons cornstarch

1 tablespoon water

1. Set the Instant Pot to sauté and add the olive oil.

2. Add the onion, garlic, paprika, parsley, and pepper to olive oil and sauté until onion starts to soften. Push onion to side of pot.

3. With the Instant Pot still at sauté, add the chicken and sear on each side for 3 to 5 minutes.

4. Mix broth, lemon juice, and salt together. Pour over chicken and stir to mix.

5. Put on lid and set Instant Pot, move vent to sealing and press Poultry. Set cook time for 7 minutes. Let depressurize naturally.

6. Remove chicken, leaving sauce in pot. Mix cornstarch in water and add to sauce. (Can start with 1 tablespoon cornstarch, and use second one if sauce isn't thick enough.)

Serving suggestion:

Serve chicken and sauce over whole wheat noodles or brown rice.

Non Pantry Staple Grocery List
2 lb. boneless chicken breasts or
    thighs
1 tablespoon fresh chopped
    parsley (or 1 teaspoon dried
    parsley)
⅓ cup lemon juice
1–2 tablespoons cornstarch

Calories 361

Fat 13 g

Saturated Fat 2 g

Cholesterol 165 mg

Sodium 639 mg

Total Carbs 7 g

Fiber 0.5 g

Protein 52 g

Mjadra (Lentils and Rice)

Hope Comerford,
Clinton Township, MI

Makes 4–6 servings
Prep. Time: 1 hour 20 minutes ⚹ *Cooking Time: 8 hours* ⚹ *Ideal slow-cooker size: 3-qt.*

½ cup olive oil

2 large sweet onions, chopped

1 cup dried lentils, rinsed

4 cups water

¼ cup lemon juice

⅛ teaspoon pepper

1 teaspoon salt

1 cup uncooked brown rice

1. Heat the olive oil over medium-high heat. Add the onions and let brown lightly. Reduce the heat to low and cover. Let the onions caramelize for at least 1 hour.

2. When the onions are done, add them and all of the remaining ingredients to the crock and stir.

3. Cover and cook for 8 hours on Low.

Serving suggestion:

Serve with whole-grain pita or on a bed of lettuce.

Non Pantry Staple Grocery List
1 cup dried lentils
¼ cup lemon juice
1 cup brown rice

Calories 398
Fat 19 g
Saturated Fat 3 g
Cholesterol 0 mg
Sodium 329 mg
Total Carbs 47 g
Fiber 5 g
Protein 11 g

Chicken with Lemon

Colleen Heatwole
Burton, MI

Makes 4 servings
Prep. Time: 15 minutes ⚜ Cooking Time: 8 minutes ⚜ Setting: Manual
Pressure: High ⚜ Release: Natural

2 lb. boneless, skinless chicken thighs

3 tablespoons olive oil, divided

1 teaspoon rosemary

1 teaspoon kosher salt

½ teaspoon black pepper

1 lemon, organic preferred

1 medium onion, diced

2 garlic cloves, minced

2 tablespoons water

1. Toss chicken with 1 tablespoon oil, rosemary, salt, and pepper.

2. Wash lemon, trim ends, quarter lengthwise, and remove seeds. Slice quarters crosswise into ⅛-inch slices.

3. Heat remaining 2 tablespoons oil using sauté function in the inner pot of the Instant Pot.

4. Add onion and garlic and sauté for 3 minutes, stirring frequently.

5. Add lemon and sauté for an additional minute.

6. Add the 2 tablespoons water.

7. Add chicken and stir to combine.

8. Secure the lid and set vent to sealing. Cook for 8 minutes, using Manual high pressure.

9. Allow pressure to release naturally.

Non Pantry Staple Grocery List
2 lb. boneless, skinless chicken thighs
1 lemon

Calories 378
Fat 16 g
Saturated Fat 2 g
Cholesterol 166 mg
Sodium 185 mg
Total Carbs 6 g
Fiber 2 g
Protein 52 g

Main Dishes ❧ 113

Lemony Chicken Thighs

Maria Shevlin
Sicklerville , NJ

Makes 3–5 servings
Prep. Time: 15 minutes ❧ *Cooking Time: 15 minutes* ❧ *Setting: Poultry*
Pressure: High ❧ *Release: Natural then Manual*

5 frozen bone-in chicken thighs

1 cup vegetable broth

Juice of 1 lemon

1 small onion, diced

5–6 garlic cloves, diced

2 Tbsp olive oil

½ teaspoon salt

¼ teaspoon black pepper

1 teaspoon True Lemon brand Lemon Pepper seasoning

1 teaspoon parsley flakes

¼ teaspoon oregano

Zest of 1 lemon for garnish

1. Add all ingredients except lemon zest to the inner pot of the Instant Pot.

2. Lock the lid, make sure the vent is in sealing position, then press the Poultry button. Set to 15 minutes.

3. When cook time is up, let the pressure naturally release for 3 to 5 minutes, then manually release the rest.

4. You can place these under the broiler for 2 to 3 minutes to brown.

5. Plate up and pour some of the sauce over the top with fresh lemon zest.

Non Pantry Staple Grocery List
5 frozen bone-in chicken thighs
1 lemon
1 teaspoon True Lemon brand lemon pepper seasoning

Calories 336
Fat 25 g
Saturated Fat 6 g
Cholesterol 142 mg
Sodium 354 mg
Total Carbs 3 g
Fiber 0 g
Protein 26 g

Lemon Pepper Chicken with Veggies

Nadine Martinitz
Salina, KS

Makes 4 servings

Prep. Time: 20 minutes & Cooking Time: 4–10 hours & Ideal slow-cooker size: 4-qt.

4 carrots, sliced ½-inch thick

4 potatoes, cut in 1-inch chunks

2 cloves garlic, peeled and minced, optional

4 whole chicken legs and thighs, skin removed

2 teaspoons lemon pepper seasoning

1 teaspoon poultry seasoning, optional

1¾ cups vegetable broth

1. Layer vegetables and chicken in slow cooker.

2. Sprinkle with lemon pepper seasoning and poultry seasoning if you wish. Pour broth over all.

3. Cover and cook on Low for 8 to 10 hours or on High for 4 to 5 hours.

Variation:

Add 2 cups frozen green beans to the bottom layer (step 1) in the cooker.
—Earnest Zimmerman, Mechanicsburg, PA

Non Pantry Staple Grocery List

4 carrots

4 potatoes

4 whole chicken legs and thighs

Calories 696

Fat 50 g

Saturated Fat 14 g

Cholesterol 120 mg

Sodium 421 mg

Total Carbs 46 g

Fiber 6 g

Protein 16 g

Honey Baked Chicken

Mary Kennell
Roanoke, IL

Makes 4 servings
Prep. Time: 15 minutes ⚘ Cooking Time: 3–6 hours ⚘ Ideal slow-cooker size: 5-qt.

4 skinless, bone-in chicken breast
halves
2 tablespoons olive oil
2 tablespoons honey
2 teaspoons prepared mustard
2 teaspoons curry powder
Salt and pepper, optional

1. Spray slow cooker with nonstick cooking spray and add chicken.

2. Mix olive oil, honey, mustard, curry powder, and optional salt and pepper together in a small bowl. Pour sauce over chicken.

3. Cover and cook on High for 3 hours, or on Low for 5 to 6 hours.

Variations:

1. Use chicken thighs instead of breasts. Drop the curry powder if you wish.
   —Cathy Boshart, Lebanon, PA

2. Use a small fryer chicken, quartered, instead of breasts or thighs.
   —Frances Kruba, Dundalk, MD

3. Instead of curry powder, use 1/2 teaspoon paprika.
   —Jena Hammond, Traverse City, MI

Non Pantry Staple Grocery List
4 skinless, bone-in chicken breast
halves
2 teaspoons prepared mustard

Calories 232
Fat 10 g
Saturated Fat 2 g
Cholesterol 83 mg
Sodium 80 mg
Total Carbs 9 g
Fiber 1 g
Protein 26 g

Poached Chicken

Mary E. Wheatley
Mashpee, MA

Makes 6 servings
Prep. Time: 15 minutes ♣ Cooking Time: 7–8 hours ♣ Ideal slow-cooker size: 4½-qt.

3-lb. whole chicken
I rib celery, cut into chunks
I carrot, sliced
I medium onion, sliced
I cup vegetable broth or water

1. Wash chicken. Pat dry with paper towels and place in slow cooker.

2. Place celery, carrot, and onion around chicken. Pour broth over all.

3. Cover and cook on Low for 7 to 8 hours, or until chicken is tender.

4. Remove chicken from pot and place on platter. When cool enough to handle, debone.

5. Strain broth into a container and chill.

6. Place chunks of meat in fridge or freezer until ready to use in salads or main dishes.

Non Pantry Staple Grocery List
3-lb. whole chicken
I rib celery
I carrot

Calories 748
Fat 67 g
Saturated Fat 19 g
Cholesterol 179 mg
Sodium 213 mg
Total Carbs 3 g
Fiber 1 g
Protein 31 g

Chicken with Vegetables

Janie Steele
Moore, OK

Makes 4 servings
Prep. Time: 10–15 minutes ♣ Cooking Time: 6–8 hours ♣ Ideal slow-cooker size: 6-qt.

4 bone-in chicken breast halves

1 small head cabbage, quartered

1 (1-lb.) bag baby carrots

2 (14½-oz.) cans Mexican-flavored stewed tomatoes

1. Place all ingredients in slow cooker in order listed.

2. Cover and cook on Low for 6 to 8 hours, or until chicken and vegetables are tender.

Non Pantry Staple Grocery List
4 bone-in chicken breast halves

Calories 409
Fat 16 g
Saturated Fat 4 g
Cholesterol 73 mg
Sodium 1088 mg
Total Carbs 39 g
Fiber 7 g
Protein 29 g

Chicken Curry with Rice

Jennifer Yoder Sommers
Harrisonburg, VA

Makes 6 servings
Prep. Time: 10 minutes ♣ Cooking Time: 5–10 hours ♣ Ideal slow-cooker size: 3- to 4-qt.

1½ lb. boneless, skinless chicken thighs,
quartered

1 onion, chopped

2 cups uncooked brown rice

2 tablespoons curry powder

1¾ cups vegetable broth

1. Combine all ingredients in your slow cooker.

2. Cover and cook on Low for 8 to 10 hours, or on High for 5 hours, or until chicken is tender but not dry.

Variation:

Thirty minutes before the end of the cooking time, stir in 2 cups frozen peas.

Non Pantry Staple Grocery List
1½ lb. boneless, skinless chicken
thighs
2 cups brown rice

Calories 371
Fat 11 g
Saturated Fat 2 g
Cholesterol 87 mg
Sodium 384 mg
Total Carbs 51 g
Fiber 4 g
Protein 26 g

Curried Chicken Dinner

Janessa Hochstedler
East Earl, PA

Makes 6 servings
Prep. Time: 20 minutes　⚶　Cooking Time: 5–10 hours　⚶　Ideal slow-cooker size: 3-qt.

1½ lb. boneless, skinless chicken thighs, quartered

3 potatoes, peeled and cut into chunks, about 2 cups

1 apple, chopped

2 tablespoons curry powder

1¾ cups vegetable broth

1 medium onion, chopped, optional

1. Place all ingredients in slow cooker. Mix gently.

2. Cover and cook on Low for 8 to 10 hours or on High for 5 hours, or until chicken is tender, but not dry.

3. Serve over cooked brown rice.

Non Pantry Staple Grocery List
1½ lb. boneless, skinless chicken thighs
3 potatoes
1 apple

Calories 315
Fat 9 g
Saturated Fat 2 g
Cholesterol 88 mg
Sodium 390 mg
Total Carbs 26 g
Fiber 4 g
Protein 23 g

Spanish Chicken

Natalia Showalter
Mt. Solon, VA

Makes 4–6 servings
Prep. Time: 15–20 minutes & Cooking Time: 5–6 hours & Ideal slow-cooker size: 3- to 6-qt.

8 chicken thighs, skinned

½–1 cup red wine vinegar, according to your taste preference

⅔ cups tamari, or low-sodium soy sauce

1 teaspoon garlic powder

4 (6-inch) cinnamon sticks

1. Brown chicken slightly in nonstick skillet, if you wish, and then transfer to greased slow cooker.

2. Mix wine vinegar, tamari, and garlic powder together in a bowl. Pour over chicken.

3. Break cinnamon sticks into several pieces and distribute among chicken thighs.

4. Cover and cook on Low for 5 to 6 hours, or until chicken is tender but not dry.

TIP
You can skip browning the chicken if you're in a hurry, but browning it gives the finished dish a better flavor.

Non Pantry Staple Grocery List
8 chicken thighs
½–1 cup red wine vinegar
⅔ cups tamari or low-sodium soy sauce
4 (6-inch) cinnamon sticks

Calories 211
Fat 12 g
Saturated Fat 3 g
Cholesterol 120 mg
Sodium 3071 mg
Total Carbs 3 g
Fiber 0 g
Protein 33 g

Easy Enchilada Shredded Chicken

Hope Comerford
Clinton Township, MI

Makes 10–14 servings
Prep. Time: 5 minutes ♣ Cooking Time: 5–6 hours ♣ Ideal slow-cooker size: 3- to 5-qt.

5–6 lb. boneless, skinless chicken breast

1 (14½-oz.) can petite diced tomatoes

1 medium onion, chopped

8 ounces red enchilada sauce

½ teaspoon salt

½ teaspoon chili powder

½ teaspoon basil

½ teaspoon garlic powder

¼ teaspoon pepper

1. Place chicken in the crock.

2. Add the remaining ingredients.

3. Cover and cook on Low for 5 to 6 hours.

4. Remove chicken and shred it between two forks. Place the shredded chicken back in the crock and stir back through the juices.

Serving suggestion:

Serve over salad, brown rice, quinoa, or sweet potatoes.

Non Pantry Staple Grocery List
5–6 lb. boneless, skinless chicken breast
1 (14½-oz.) can petite diced tomatoes
8 ounces red enchilada sauce

Calories 251
Fat 7 g
Saturated Fat 2 g
Cholesterol 136 mg
Sodium 339 mg
Total Carbs 3 g
Fiber 0 g
Protein 42 g

Filled Acorn Squash

Teresa Martin
New Hlland, PA

Makes 4 servings
Prep. Time: 20–30 minutes   Cooking Time: 5–11 hours   Ideal slow-cooker size: 7-qt.

2 medium acorn squash, about 1 ¼ lb. each

2 tablespoons water

1 (15-oz.) can black beans, drained, rinsed

½ cup pine nuts, raw, or toasted if you have time

1 large tomato, coarsely chopped

2 scallions, thinly sliced

1 teaspoon ground cumin

½ teaspoon black pepper, divided

2 teaspoons olive oil

½ cup reduced-fat shredded Monterey Jack cheese, optional

Non Pantry Staple Grocery List

2 medium acorn squash (about 1 ¼ lb. each)

1 (15-oz.) can black beans

½ cup pine nuts, raw

1 large tomato

2 scallions

½ cup reduced-fat shredded Monterey Jack cheese, optional

Calories 440

Fat 20 g

Saturated Fat 6 g

Cholesterol 20 mg

Sodium 180 mg

Total Carbs 52 g

Fiber 14 g

Protein 21 g

1. Grease interior of slow-cooker crock.

2. Place washed whole squashes in slow cooker. Spoon in water.

3. Cover and cook on High for 4 to 6 hours or on Low for 7 to 9 hours, or until squashes jag tender when you pierce them with a fork.

4. While squashes are cooking, mix beans, pine nuts, tomato, scallions, cumin, and ¼ teaspoon black pepper. Set aside.

5. Use sturdy tongs or wear oven mitts to lift squashes out of cooker. Let cool until you can cut them in half and scoop out the seeds.

6. Brush cut sides and cavity of each squash half with olive oil.

7. Sprinkle all four cut sides with remaining black pepper.

8. Spoon heaping ½ cup of bean mixture into each halved squash, pressing down gently to fill cavity.

9. Return halves to slow cooker. Cover and cook on High for another hour, or on Low for another 2 hours, until vegetables are as tender as you like them and thoroughly hot.

10. Uncover and sprinkle with optional cheese just before serving. When cheese has melted, put a filled half squash on each diner's plate.

Eggplant Italian

Melanie Thrower
McPherson, KS

Makes 6–8 servings
Prep. Time: 30 minutes ⚜ Cooking Time: 4 hours
Ideal slow-cooker size: 4- or 5-qt. (an oval cooker works best)

2 eggplants

¼ cup Egg Beaters

24 ounces fat-free cottage cheese

¼ teaspoon salt

Black pepper to taste

1 (14-oz.) can tomato sauce

2–4 tablespoons Italian seasoning, according to your taste preference

1. Peel eggplants and cut in ½-inch-thick slices. Soak in salt water for about 5 minutes to remove bitterness. Drain well.

2. Spray slow cooker with fat-free cooking spray.

3. Mix Egg Beaters, cottage cheese, salt, and pepper together in a bowl.

4. Mix tomato sauce and Italian seasoning together in another bowl.

5. Spoon a thin layer of tomato sauce into bottom of slow cooker. Top with about one-third of eggplant slices, and then one-third of egg/cheese mixture, and finally one-third of remaining tomato sauce mixture.

6. Repeat those layers twice, ending with seasoned tomato sauce.

7. Cover. Cook on High for 4 hours. Allow to rest for 15 minutes before serving.

Non Pantry Staple Grocery List
2 eggplants
¼ cup Egg Beaters
24 ounces fat-free cottage cheese
1 (14-oz.) can tomato sauce

Calories 119
Fat 2 g
Saturated Fat 1 g
Cholesterol 10 mg
Sodium 574 mg
Total Carbs 14 g
Fiber 5 g
Protein 12 g

Baked Ziti

Hope Comerford
Clinton Township, MI

Makes 8 servings
Prep. Time: 15 minutes   ❧   Cooking Time: 4 hours   ❧   Ideal slow-cooker size: 5-qt.

1 (28-oz.) can low-sodium crushed tomatoes

1 (15-oz.) can low-sodium tomato sauce

1½ teaspoons Italian seasoning

1 teaspoon garlic powder

1 teaspoon onion powder

1 teaspoon pepper

1 teaspoon sea salt

1 lb. whole wheat ziti or rigatoni pasta, uncooked, divided

1 cup low-fat shredded mozzarella cheese, divided

1. Spray crock with nonstick spray.

2. In a bowl, mix crushed tomatoes, tomato sauce, Italian seasoning, garlic powder, onion powder, pepper, and salt.

3. In the bottom of the crock, pour ⅓ of the pasta sauce.

4. Add ½ of the pasta on top of the sauce.

5. Add another ⅓ of your pasta sauce.

6. Spread ½ of the mozzarella cheese on top of that.

7. Add the remaining pasta, the remaining sauce, and the remaining cheese on top of that.

8. Cover and cook on Low for 4 hours.

Non Pantry Staple Grocery List

1 (28-oz.) can low-sodium crushed tomatoes

1 (15-oz.) can low-sodium tomato sauce

1 lb. whole wheat ziti or rigatoni pasta

1 cup low-fat shredded Mozzarella cheese

Calories 398
Fat 11 g
Saturated Fat 6 g
Cholesterol 30 mg
Sodium 1054 mg
Total Carbs 54 g
Fiber 4 g
Protein 23 g

Faked You Out Alfredo

Sue Hamilton
Benson, AZ

Makes 4 servings
Prep. Time: 5 minutes ❧ Cooking Time: 6 hours ❧ Ideal slow-cooker size: 3-qt.

1 (1-lb.) bag frozen cauliflower

1 (13½-oz.) can light coconut milk

½ cup diced onion

2 cloves garlic, minced

1 tablespoon vegetable concentrated bouillon base

Salt and pepper to taste

1. Place the frozen cauliflower, coconut milk, onion, garlic, and the vegetable bouillon concentrate in your crock. Stir mixture to blend in the stock concentrate.

2. Cover and cook on Low for 6 hours.

3. Place cooked mixture in blender and process until smooth.

4. Add salt and pepper to taste.

Serving suggestion:

Serve over cooked pasta, cooked sliced potatoes, or any other vegetable.

TIP

"My husband loves this on pasta with cooked mushrooms mixed in. This sauce can be made ahead of time and refrigerated."

Non Pantry Staple Grocery List
1 (1-lb.) bag frozen cauliflower
1 (13½-oz.) can light coconut milk
1 tablespoon vegetable
  concentrated bouillon base

Calories 92
Fat 6 g
Saturated Fat 5 g
Cholesterol 0 mg
Sodium 663 mg
Total Carbs 7 g
Fiber 1 g
Protein 3 g

Vegetable Stuffed Peppers

Shirley Hinh
Wayland, IA

Makes 8 servings
Prep. Time: 20 minutes ⅍ Cooking Time: 6–8 hours ⅍ Ideal slow-cooker size: 6-qt.

4 large green, red, orange, or yellow bell peppers

½ cup brown rice

¼ cup minced onions

¼ cup sliced black olives

2 teaspoons liquid aminos

¼ teaspoon black pepper

1 clove garlic, minced

1 (28-oz.) can low-sodium whole tomatoes

1 (6-oz.) can low-sodium tomato paste

1 (15¼-oz.) can kidney beans, drained, rinsed

1. Cut tops off peppers (reserve) and remove seeds. Stand peppers up in slow cooker.

2. Mix remaining ingredients in a bowl. Stuff peppers. (You'll have leftover filling.)

3. Place pepper tops back on peppers. Pour remaining filling over the stuffed peppers and work down in between the peppers.

4. Cover and cook on Low for 6 to 8 hours, or until the peppers are done to your liking.

5. If you prefer, you may add ½ cup tomato juice if recipe is too dry.

6. Cut peppers in half and serve.

Non Pantry Staple Grocery List

4 large bell peppers (colors of your choice)

½ cup brown rice

¼ cup sliced black olives

2 teaspoons liquid aminos or tamari

1 (28-oz.) can low-sodium whole tomatoes

1 (6-oz.) can low-sodium tomato paste

1 (15¼-oz.) can kidney beans

Calories 198
Fat 4 g
Saturated Fat 1 g
Cholesterol 0 mg
Sodium 3 mg
Total Carbs 547 g
Fiber 8 g
Protein 9 g

Zucchini Vegetable Pot

Edwina Stoltzfus
Narvon, PA

Makes 6 servings
Prep. Time: 40 minutes   Cooking Time: 3–4 hours   Ideal slow-cooker size: 3½- or 4-qt.

1 lb. lean ground turkey or meatless crumbles

2 cups diced zucchini

2 ribs celery, chopped

¼ cup chopped green bell pepper

1 large onion, chopped

2 large tomatoes, chopped

¼ cup brown rice, uncooked

¾ teaspoon sea salt

¼ teaspoon garlic powder

⅛ teaspoon nutmeg

¼ teaspoon black pepper

1 teaspoon Worcestershire sauce

1. Brown turkey in nonstick skillet. If using meatless crumbles, skip this step and replace the turkey with the crumbles in the following step.

2. Meanwhile, place vegetables in slow cooker. Top with rice and ground turkey.

3. Sprinkle seasonings over the top.

4. Cover and cook on High for 3 to 4 hours.

Non Pantry Staple Grocery List
1 lb. lean ground turkey or meatless crumbles
2 cups diced zucchini
2 ribs celery
¼ cup chopped green bell pepper
2 large tomatoes
¼ cup brown rice
1 teaspoon Worcestershire sauce

Calories 153
Fat 6 g
Saturated Fat 2 g
Cholesterol 172 mg
Sodium 3 mg
Total Carbs 11 g
Fiber 3 g
Protein 16 g

Tofu "Spaghetti" Quinoa

Hope Comerford
Clinton Township, MI

Makes 8–10 servings
Prep. Time: 5 minutes ⚶ Cooking Time: 5 hours ⚶ Ideal slow-cooker size: 5- or 6-qt.

2 lb. meatless crumbles

½ teaspoon salt

⅛ teaspoon pepper

I teaspoon garlic powder

I teaspoon onion powder

I cup quinoa

I cup chopped onion

I cup low-fat shredded mozzarella cheese

4 cups tomato sauce

2 cups water

1. Spray crock with nonstick spray.

2. Place all ingredients in crock and stir.

3. Cover and cook on Low for 5 hours.

Non Pantry Staple Grocery List

2 lb. meatless crumbles

I cup quinoa

I cup low-fat shredded mozzarella cheese

4 cups tomato sauce

Calories 223
Fat 4 g
Saturated Fat 1 g
Cholesterol 7 mg
Sodium 1069 mg
Total Carbs 28 g
Fiber 8 g
Protein 27 g

Spaghetti with No-Meat Sauce

Becky Fixel
Grosse Pointe Farms, MI

Makes 6–8 servings
Prep. Time: 5 minutes   ☙   Cooking Time: 6 hours   ☙   Ideal slow-cooker size: 7-qt.

2 tablespoons olive oil

1 (28-oz.) can crushed tomatoes

1 (28-oz.) can tomato sauce

1 (15-oz.) can Italian stewed tomatoes

1 (6-oz.) can tomato paste

2–3 tablespoons basil

2 tablespoons oregano

2 tablespoons honey

2 tablespoons garlic paste (or 2 large cloves, peeled and minced)

2 lb. meatless crumbles

1. Pour olive oil in the crock. Use a paper towel to rub it all around the inside.

2. Add all ingredients to crock. Mix.

3. Cover and cook on Low for 6 hours.

Serving suggestion:

Serve over your favorite whole wheat pasta.

Non Pantry Staple Grocery List
1 (28-oz.) can crushed tomatoes
1 (28-oz.) can tomato sauce
1 (15-oz.) can Italian stewed tomatoes
1 (6-oz.) can tomato paste
2 tablespoons garlic paste
2 lb. meatless crumbles

Calories 295
Fat 6 g
Saturated Fat 1 g
Cholesterol 0 mg
Sodium 1659 mg
Total Carbs 40 g
Fiber 12 g
Protein 32 g

Mexi Rotini

Jane Geigley
Lancaster, PA

Makes 6 servings
Prep. Time: 30 minutes ⚜ Cooking Time: 4½ hours ⚜ Ideal slow-cooker size: 4-qt.

1 cup water

3 cups partially cooked whole wheat rotini

1 (12-oz.) package frozen mixed vegetables

1 (10-oz.) can Ro*Tel diced tomatoes with green chilies

1 (4-oz.) can green chilies, undrained

1 lb. meatless crumbles

½ cup low-fat shredded cheddar cheese

1. Combine all ingredients in slow cooker except shredded cheddar.

2. Cover and cook on Low for 4 hours.

3. Top with the low-fat shredded cheddar, then let cook covered for an additional 20 minutes or so.

Non Pantry Staple Grocery List
3 cups whole wheat rotini
1 (12-oz.) package frozen mixed vegetables
1 (10-oz.) can Ro*Tel diced tomatoes with green chilies
1 (4-oz.) can green chilies
1 lb. meatless crumbles
1 cup low-fat shredded cheddar cheese

Calories 239
Fat 2g
Saturated Fat 0.5 g
Cholesterol 2 mg
Sodium 852 mg
Total Carbs 38 g
Fiber 8 g
Protein 26 g

Asian-Style Tempeh with Pineapple

Andrea Maher
Dunedin, FL

Makes 6 servings
Prep. Time: 10 minutes ❧ *Cooking Time: 6 hours* ❧ *Ideal slow-cooker size: 5- or 6-qt.*

24 ounces tempeh, sliced into strips

3 cups pineapple, cubed

¼ cup liquid aminos

1 tablespoon honey

½ cup chopped onion or 2 tablespoons onion powder

1 cup vegetable stock

½ teaspoon ground ginger

2 (16-oz.) bags frozen Szechuan mixed veggies (or any mixed veggies)

1. Add all ingredients except frozen veggies to the slow cooker.

2. Cover and cook on Low for 6 hours.

3. Add frozen veggies in the last 1 to 2 hours.

Non Pantry Staple Grocery List

24 ounces tempeh

3 cups cubed pineapple

¼ cup liquid aminos

2 (16-oz.) bags frozen Szechuan mixed veggies (or any mixed veggies)

Calories 370
Fat 8 g
Saturated Fat 2 g
Cholesterol 0 mg
Sodium 456 mg
Total Carbs 47 g
Fiber 18 g
Protein 27 g

Tofu and Vegetables

Donna Lantgen
Rapid City, SD

Makes 4 servings
Prep. Time: 25–30 minutes ⚶ Cooking Time: 6 hours ⚶ Ideal slow-cooker size: 4- or 5-qt.

1 lb. firm tofu, drained and crumbled
½ cup chopped onion
½ cup chopped celery
2 cups chopped bok choy
2 cups chopped napa cabbage
½ cup pea pods, cut in half
¼ cup liquid aminos or coconut aminos

1. Combine all ingredients in slow cooker.

2. Cook on Low for 6 hours.

Serving suggestion:
This is wonderful served on a bed of brown rice.

Non Pantry Staple Grocery List
1 lb. firm tofu
½ cup chopped celery
2 cups chopped bok choy
2 cups chopped napa cabbage
½ cup pea pods
¼ cup liquid aminos or coconut aminos

Calories 128
Fat 5 g
Saturated Fat 1 g
Cholesterol 0 mg
Sodium 224 mg
Total Carbs 12 g
Fiber 2 g
Protein 12 g

Juicy Orange Tempeh

Andrea Maher
Dunedin, FL

Makes 6 servings
Prep. Time: 10 minutes ⚜ Cooking Time: 6 hours ⚜ Ideal slow-cooker size: 5- or 6-qt.

18–24 ounces tempeh, cut into strips

1 cup orange juice

¼ cup honey

6 small oranges, peeled and sliced

¼ cup liquid aminos

6 cups broccoli slaw

1. Add all the ingredients to the slow cooker except the broccoli slaw.

2. Cover and cook on Low for 6 hours.

3. Divide mixture between 6 mason jars.

4. Add 1 cup broccoli slaw to each mason jar.

5. Pour into a bowl when you're ready to eat!

Non Pantry Staple Grocery List

18–24 ounces tempeh

1 cup orange juice

6 small oranges

¼ cup liquid aminos

6 cups broccoli slaw

Calories 361
Fat 8 g
Saturated Fat 2 g
Cholesterol 0 mg
Sodium 152 mg
Total Carbs 48 g
Fiber 16 g
Protein 26 g

Plant-Based Kielbasa and Cabbage

Mary Ann Lefever
Lancaster, PA

Makes 4 servings
Prep. Time: 10–15 minutes ☙ *Cooking Time: 6–8 hours* ☙ *Ideal slow-cooker size: 4- or 5-qt.*

1 lb. plant-based kielbasa sausage, cut into 4 chunks

4 large white potatoes, cut into chunks

1-lb. head green cabbage, shredded

1 qt. whole tomatoes (strained if you don't like seeds)

1 medium onion, thinly sliced, optional

1. Layer kielbasa, then potatoes, and then cabbage into slow cooker.

2. Pour tomatoes over the top.

3. Top with sliced onion if you wish.

4. Cover. Cook on Low for 6 to 8 hours, or until vegetables are as tender as you like them.

Non Pantry Staple Grocery List
1 lb. plant-based kielbasa sausage
4 large white potatoes
1 lb. head green cabbage
1 qt. whole tomatoes

Calories 527
Fat 22 g
Saturated Fat 4 g
Cholesterol 0 mg
Sodium 1321 mg
Total Carbs 65 g
Fiber 15 g
Protein 29 g

Savory Red Beans and Rice

Arianne Hochstetler
Goshen, IN

Makes 10–12 servings
Prep. Time: 15 minutes & Cooking Time: 4½–5½ hours & Ideal slow-cooker size: 6-qt.

1 (16-oz.) package dry kidney beans, sorted and rinsed

1 large green bell pepper, chopped

1 cup chopped onions

2 garlic cloves, minced

7 cups water

1½ teaspoons salt

¼ teaspoon pepper

2 cups uncooked instant brown rice

Hot pepper sauce, optional

Salsa, optional

Low-fat sour cream, optional

1. In a 4- or 6-qt. slow cooker, combine beans, pepper, onions, garlic, water, salt, and pepper.

2. Cover. Cook on High for 4 to 5 hours.

3. Stir instant brown rice into bean mixture.

4. Cover. Cook on High for an additional 15 to 20 minutes.

5. Serve with optional hot pepper sauce, salsa, and low-fat sour cream.

TIP
I like to sauté the peppers, onions, and garlic before adding them to the slow cooker.

Non Pantry Staple Grocery List
1 (16-oz.) package dry kidney beans
1 large green bell pepper
2 cups instant brown rice
Hot pepper sauce
Salsa and sour cream

Calories 246
Fat 1 g
Saturated Fat 0 g
Cholesterol 0 mg
Sodium 256 mg
Total Carbs 48 g
Fiber 11 g
Protein 11 g

Side Dishes and Vegetables

Broccoli and Bell Peppers

Frieda Weisz
Aberdeen, SD

Makes 8 servings
Prep. Time: 20 minutes & Cooking Time: 4–5 hours & Ideal slow-cooker size: 3½- or 4-qt.

2 lb. fresh broccoli, trimmed and chopped into bite-size pieces

1 clove garlic, minced

1 bell pepper, cut into thin slices

1 onion, cut into slices

4 tablespoons liquid aminos

½ teaspoon salt

Dash black pepper

1 tablespoon sesame seeds, optional, as garnish

1. Combine all ingredients except sesame seeds in slow cooker.

2. Cook on Low for 4 to 5 hours. Top with sesame seeds.

3. Serve on brown rice.

Non Pantry Staple Grocery List
2 lb. fresh broccoli
1 bell pepper
4 tablespoons liquid aminos
1 tablespoon sesame seeds, optional

Calories 20
Fat 0.5 g
Saturated Fat 0 g
Cholesterol 0 mg
Sodium 459 mg
Total Carbs 4 g
Fiber 1 g
Protein 2 g

Italian Broccoli

Linda Gebo
Plattsburgh, NY

Makes 4 servings
Prep. Time: 25–30 minutes ⚭ *Cooking Time: 10–15 minutes*

1 large head broccoli

1 clove garlic

½ cup water

1 tablespoon, or more, vegetable broth

Salt and pepper to taste

1 (2-oz.) jar pimientos

1. Remove leaves and peel lower part of broccoli stalks. Cut into florets and ½-inch slices.

2. Steam cut-up broccoli and whole garlic clove in water in skillet for about 4 minutes. Discard garlic and add broth.

3. Salt and pepper to taste.

4. Cover and cook over low heat 10 to 15 minutes, or until broccoli is tender. You may need to add more broth if skillet gets dry.

5. Sprinkle with pimientos and serve.

Non Pantry Staple Grocery List
1 large head of broccoli
1 (2-oz.) jar pimientos

Calories 59
Fat 1 g
Saturated Fat 0.5 g
Cholesterol 3 mg
Sodium 257 mg
Total Carbs 9 g
Fiber 3 g
Protein 4 g

Potatoes with Parsley

Colleen Heatwole
Burton, MI

Makes 4 servings
Prep. Time: 10 minutes ❧ Cooking Time: 5 minutes ❧ Setting: Manual
Pressure: High ❧ Release: Manual

3 tablespoons olive oil, divided

2 lb. medium red potatoes (about 2 ounces each), halved lengthwise

1 garlic clove, minced

½ teaspoon salt

½ cup vegetable broth

2 tablespoons chopped fresh parsley

1. Place 1 tablespoon olive oil in the inner pot of the Instant Pot and select sauté.

2. When olive oil is hot, add potatoes, garlic, and salt, stirring well.

3. Sauté for 4 minutes, stirring frequently.

4. Add vegetable broth and stir well.

5. Seal lid, make sure vent is on sealing, then select manual for 5 minutes on High.

6. When cooking time is up, manually release the pressure.

7. Strain potatoes toss with remaining 2 tablespoons olive oil and chopped parsley. Serve immediately.

Non Pantry Staple Grocery List
2 lb. medium red potatoes
2 tablespoons chopped fresh
    parsley

Calories 251
Fat 11 g
Saturated Fat 1.5 g
Cholesterol 0 mg
Sodium 289 mg
Total Carbs 36 g
Fiber 4 g
Protein 4.5 g

Greek-Style Green Beans

Diann J. Dunham
State College, PA

Makes 6 servings
Prep. Time: 5 minutes & Cooking Time: 2–5 hours & Ideal slow-cooker size: 4-qt.

20 ounces whole or cut-up frozen green beans (not French cut)

2 cups low-sodium tomato sauce

2 teaspoons dried onion flakes, optional

Pinch dried marjoram or oregano

Pinch ground nutmeg

Pinch cinnamon

1. Combine all ingredients in slow cooker, mixing together thoroughly.

2. Cover and cook on Low for 2 to 4 hours if the beans are defrosted, or for 3 to 5 hours on Low if the beans are frozen, or until the beans are done to your liking.

Non Pantry Staple Grocery List
20 ounces whole or cut-up frozen green beans
2 cups low-sodium tomato sauce

Calories 47
Fat 0.5 g
Saturated Fat 0 g
Cholesterol 0 mg
Sodium 386 mg
Total Carbs 11 g
Fiber 4 g
Protein 2 g

Lemony Garlic Asparagus

Hope Comerford
Clinton Township, MI

Makes 4 servings
Prep. Time: 5 minutes & Cooking Time: 1½–2 hours & Ideal slow-cooker size: 2- or 3-qt.

1 lb. asparagus, bottom inch (hard part) removed

1 tablespoon olive oil

1½ tablespoon lemon juice

3–4 cloves garlic, minced

¼ teaspoon salt

⅛ teaspoon pepper

1. Spray crock with nonstick spray.

2. Lay asparagus at bottom of crock and coat with the olive oil.

3. Pour the lemon juice over the top, then sprinkle with the garlic, salt, and pepper.

4. Cover and cook on Low for 1½ to 2 hours.

Non Pantry Staple Grocery List
1 lb. asparagus
1½ tablespoons lemon juice

Calories 58
Fat 4 g
Saturated Fat 0.5 g
Cholesterol 0 mg
Sodium 122 mg
Total Carbs 6 g
Fiber 2 g
Protein 3 g

Artichokes

Susan Yoder Graber
Eureka, IL

Makes 4 servings
Prep. Time: 20 minutes ♣ *Cooking Time: 2–10 hours* ♣ *Ideal slow-cooker size: 3-qt.*

4 artichokes

1 teaspoon salt

2 tablespoons lemon juice

1. Wash and trim artichokes by cutting off the stems flush with the bottoms of the artichokes and by cutting ¾–1 inch off the tops. Stand upright in slow cooker.

2. Mix salt and lemon juice and pour over artichokes.

3. Pour in water to cover ¾ of artichokes.

4. Cover. Cook on Low for 8 to 10 hours or on High for 2 to 4 hours.

Non Pantry Staple Grocery List
4 artichokes
2 tablespoons lemon juice

Calories 62
Fat 0 g
Saturated Fat 0 g
Cholesterol 0 mg
Sodium 600 mg
Total Carbs 14 g
Fiber 7 g
Protein 4 g

Slow-Cooked Glazed Carrots

Michele Ruvola
Selden, NY

Makes 6–7 servings
Prep. Time: 5 minutes ⚬ *Cooking Time: 6½–8½ hours* ⚬ *Ideal slow-cooker size: 3- to 4-qt.*

1 (2-lb.) bag baby carrots
1½ cups water
¼ cup honey
2 tablespoons olive oil
¼ teaspoon salt
⅛ teaspoon pepper

1. Combine carrots and water in slow cooker.

2. Cover and cook on Low for 6 to 8 hours, or until carrots are tender.

3. Drain carrots and return to slow cooker.

4. Stir in honey, olive oil, salt, and pepper. Mix well.

5. Cover and cook on Low for 30 minutes, or until glazed.

Non Pantry Staple Grocery List
1 (2-lb.) bag baby carrots

Calories 124
Fat 4 g
Saturated Fat 0.5 g
Cholesterol 0 mg
Sodium 160 mg
Total Carbs 22 g
Fiber 4 g
Protein 1 g

Corn on the Cob

Donna Conto
Saylorsburg, PA

Makes 3–4 servings
Prep. Time: 10 minutes ⚜ *Cooking Time: 2–3 hours* ⚜ *Ideal slow-cooker size: 5- or 6-qt.*

6–8 ears of corn (in husk)
½ cup water

1. Remove silk from corn, as much as possible, but leave husks on.

2. Cut off ends of corn so ears can stand in the cooker.

3. Add water.

4. Cover. Cook on Low for 2 to 3 hours.

Non Pantry Staple Grocery List
6–8 ears of corn

Calories 155
Fat 2 g
Saturated Fat 0.5 g
Cholesterol 0 mg
Sodium 27 mg
Total Carbs 34 g
Fiber 4 g
Protein 6 g

Wild Mushrooms Italian

Connie Johnson
Loudon, NH

Makes 4–5 servings
Prep. Time: 20 minutes ❧ *Cooking Time: 6–8 hours* ❧ *Ideal slow-cooker size: 5-qt.*

2 large onions, chopped

3 large red bell peppers, chopped

3 large green bell peppers, chopped

2–3 tablespoons olive oil

1 (12-oz.) package oyster mushrooms, cleaned and chopped

4 garlic cloves, minced

3 fresh bay leaves

10 fresh basil leaves, chopped

1 tablespoon salt

1½ teaspoons pepper

1 (28-oz.) can Italian plum tomatoes, crushed, or chopped

1. Sauté onions and peppers in olive oil in skillet until soft. Stir in mushrooms and garlic. Sauté just until mushrooms begin to turn brown. Pour into slow cooker.

2. Add remaining ingredients. Stir well.

3. Cover. Cook on Low for 6 to 8 hours.

Non Pantry Staple Grocery List
3 large red bell peppers
3 large green bell peppers
1 (12-oz.) package oyster mushrooms
10 fresh basil leaves
3 fresh bay leaves
1 (28-oz.) can Italian plum tomatoes, crushed or chopped

Calories 167
Fat 9 g
Saturated Fat 1 g
Cholesterol 0 mg
Sodium 1353 mg
Total Carbs 21 g
Fiber 8 g
Protein 5 g

Side Dishes and Vegetables ❧ 171

Slow-Cooker Beets

Hope Comerford
Clinton Township, MI

Makes 4–6 servings
Prep. Time: 10 minutes ⸪ Cooking Time: 3–4 hours ⸪ Ideal slow-cooker size: 3-qt.

4–6 large beets, scrubbed well and tops removed

3 tablespoons olive oil

1 teaspoon sea salt

¼ teaspoon pepper

3 tablespoons balsamic vinegar

1 tablespoon lemon juice

1. Use foil to make a packet around each beet.

2. Divide the olive oil, salt and pepper, balsamic vinegar, and lemon juice evenly between each packet.

3. Place each beet packet into the slow cooker.

4. Cover and cook on Low for 3 to 4 hours, or until the beets are tender when poked with a knife.

5. Remove each beet packet from the crock and allow to cool and let the steam escape. Once cool enough to handle, gently peel the skin off each beet with a paring knife cut into bite-size pieces and serve with juice from the packet over the top.

Non Pantry Staple Grocery List

4–6 large beets

3 tablespoons balsamic vinegar

1 tablespoon lemon juice

Calories 103
Fat 7 g
Saturated Fat 1 g
Cholesterol 0 mg
Sodium 426 mg
Total Carbs 10 g
Fiber 2 g
Protein 2 g

Side Dishes and Vegetables 173

Brussels Sprouts and Pimientos

Donna Lantgon
Rapid City, SD

Makes 8 servings
Prep. Time: 10 minutes & Cooking Time: 6 hours & Ideal slow-cooker size: 3½- or 4-qt.

2 lb. brussels sprouts
¼ teaspoon dried oregano
½ teaspoon dried basil
1 (2-oz.) jar pimientos, drained
1 small can sliced black olives, drained
1 tablespoon olive oil
½ cup water

1. Combine all ingredients in slow cooker.

2. Cook on Low for 6 hours, or until sprouts are just tender.

Non Pantry Staple Grocery List
2 lb. brussels sprouts
1 (2-oz.) jar pimientos
1 small can sliced black olives

Calories 26
Fat 3 g
Saturated Fat 0.5 g
Cholesterol 0 mg
Sodium 60 mg
Total Carbs 1 g
Fiber 5 g
Protein 4 g

Cabbage and Potatoes

Deb Kepiro
Strasburg, PA

Makes 4 servings
Prep. Time: 15 minutes ⚜ *Cooking Time: 3–6 hours* ⚜ *Ideal slow-cooker size: 5-qt.*

1 small head cabbage, cut into thin slices

12–14 baby potatoes, cut into 1-inch chunks

10–12 whole cloves garlic

¼ cup olive oil

2 tablespoons balsamic vinegar

1 teaspoon kosher salt

½ teaspoon black pepper

1. Put cabbage, potatoes, and garlic cloves in slow cooker.

2. Add oil, vinegar, salt, and pepper.

3. Toss with hands or a spoon to coat thoroughly.

4. Cover. Cook on High for 3 hours or Low for 4 to 6 hours. The vegetables are done when the potatoes and cabbage are both as tender as you like them.

Non Pantry Staple Grocery List
1 small head cabbage
12–14 baby potatoes
2 tablespoons balsamic vinegar

Calories 319
Fat 14 g
Saturated Fat 2 g
Cholesterol 0 mg
Sodium 506 mg
Total Carbs 45 g
Fiber 5 g
Protein 5 g

Perfect "Instant" Sweet Potatoes

Brittney Horst
Lititz, PA

Makes 4–6 servings
Prep. Time: 5 minutes ❦ *Cooking Time: 15 minutes* ❦ *Setting: Manual*
Pressure: High ❦ *Release: Natural*

4–6 medium sweet potatoes

1 cup of water

1. Scrub skin of sweet potatoes with a brush until clean. Pour water into inner pot of the Instant Pot. Place steamer basket in the bottom of the inner pot. Place sweet potatoes on top of steamer basket.

2. Secure the lid and turn valve to seal.

3. Select the manual mode and set to pressure cook on High for 15 minutes.

4. Allow pressure to release naturally, which takes about 10 minutes.

5. Once the pressure valve lowers, remove lid and serve immediately.

NOTE
You can also store in the fridge for 3 to 4 days in an airtight container.

Non Pantry Staple Grocery List
4–6 medium sweet potatoes

Calories 114
Fat 0 g
Saturated Fat 0 g
Cholesterol 0 mg
Sodium 74 mg
Total Carbs 27 g
Fiber 4 g
Protein 2 g

Moroccan Sweet Potato Medley

Pat Bishop
Bedminster, PA

Makes 6 servings
Prep. Time: 20 minutes ❧ Cooking Time: 2¼–3¼ hours ❧ Ideal slow-cooker size: 4-qt.

1 medium onion, sliced
2 teaspoons olive oil
2 cloves garlic, minced
1½ teaspoons ground coriander
1½ teaspoons cumin
¼ teaspoon cayenne pepper
2 medium sweet potatoes, peeled, cut into ½-inch slices, and cooked, or canned sweet potatoes, drained
1 (14-oz.) can stewed tomatoes
¾ cup uncooked bulgur
2¼ cups water
1 (15-oz.) can chickpeas, rinsed and drained
½ cup raisins
1 cup fresh cilantro leaves

1. Sauté onion in oil in small skillet until onion is tender.

2. Combine with garlic, coriander, cumin, cayenne pepper, sweet potatoes, tomatoes, bulgur, and water in 4-qt. slow cooker.

3. Cover. Cook on Low for 2 to 3 hours, or until water is absorbed.

4. Stir in chickpeas, raisins, and cilantro. Cook 15 more minutes.

5. Serve.

TIP
Adjust the amount of cayenne pepper to suit your taste.

Non Pantry Staple Grocery List
2 medium sweet potatoes
1 (14-oz.) can stewed tomatoes
¾ cup bulgur
1 (15-oz.) can chickpeas
½ cup raisins
1 cup fresh cilantro leaves

Calories 326
Fat 6 g
Saturated Fat 1 g
Cholesterol 0 mg
Sodium 340 mg
Total Carbs 61 g
Fiber 11 g
Protein 11 g

"Baked" Sweet Potatoes

Hope Comerford
Clinton Township, MI

Makes 5 potatoes
Prep. Time: 2 minutes ⚬ *Cooking Time: 4–5 hours* ⚬ *Ideal slow-cooker size: 5- or 6-qt.*

5 sweet potatoes, pierced in several places with a fork or knife

1. Place sweet potatoes in slow cooker.

2. Cover and cook on Low for 4 to 5 hours, or when they are nice and tender when poked with a fork or knife.

Non Pantry Staple Grocery List
5 sweet potatoes

Calories 114
Fat 0 g
Saturated Fat 0 g
Cholesterol 0 mg
Sodium 73 mg
Total Carbs 27 g
Fiber 4 g
Protein 2 g

Sweet Potato Puree

Colleen Heatwole
Burton, MI

Makes 4–6 servings
Prep. Time: 10 minutes   ❧   Cooking Time: 6 minutes   ❧   Setting: Manual
Pressure: High   ❧   Release: Manual

3 lb. sweet potatoes, peeled and cut into roughly 2-inch cubes

1 cup water

2 tablespoons olive oil

1 teaspoon salt

2 teaspoons honey

2 teaspoons lemon juice

½ teaspoon cinnamon

⅛ teaspoon nutmeg, optional

1. Place sweet potatoes and water in the inner pot of the Instant Pot.

2. Secure the lid, make sure vent is at sealing, then cook for 6 minutes on High, using the manual setting.

3. Manually release the pressure when cook time is up.

4. Drain sweet potatoes and place in large mixing bowl. Mash with potato masher or hand mixer.

5. Once thoroughly mashed, add remaining ingredients.

6. Taste and adjust seasonings to taste.

7. Serve immediately while still hot.

Non Pantry Staple Grocery List
3 lb. sweet potatoes
2 teaspoons lemon juice

Calories 244
Fat 5 g
Saturated Fat 1 g
Cholesterol 0 mg
Sodium 446 mg
Total Carbs 48 g
Fiber 7 g
Protein 4 g

Autumn Sweet Potatoes

Melinda Wenger
Middleburg, PA

Makes 4 servings
Prep. Time: 20 minutes & Cooking Time: 2–3 hours & Ideal slow-cooker size: 4-qt.

4 medium sweet potatoes, peeled, sliced thinly

1 large Granny Smith apple, peeled and diced

½ cup raisins

Zest and juice of ½ orange

2 tablespoons honey

Toasted, chopped walnuts, for serving, optional

1. Place sweet potatoes in lightly greased slow cooker.

2. Top with apple, raisins, and orange zest. Drizzle with honey and orange juice.

3. Cover and cook on High for 2 to 3 hours, until sweet potatoes are tender. Serve sprinkled with walnuts if you wish.

Non Pantry Staple Grocery List
4 medium sweet potatoes
1 large Granny Smith apple
½ cup raisins
½ an orange
Toasted chopped walnuts, optional

Calories 231
Fat 0 g
Saturated Fat 0 g
Cholesterol 0 mg
Sodium 76 mg
Total Carbs 57 g
Fiber 6 g
Protein 3 g

White Beans with Sun-Dried Tomatoes

Steven Lantz
Denver, CO

Makes 4–6 servings
Prep. Time: 15 minutes ♣ Cooking Time: 4–6 hours ♣ Ideal slow-cooker size: 4-qt.

2 cups uncooked great northern beans, rinsed

2 cloves garlic, minced or pressed

1 onion, chopped

6 cups water

½ teaspoon salt

⅛ teaspoon pepper

1 cup chopped sun-dried tomatoes in oil, drained

1 (2-oz.) can sliced black olives, drained

¼ cup low-fat grated Parmesan cheese

1. Mix all ingredients except tomatoes, olives, and cheese in 4- or 5-qt. slow cooker.

2. Cover and cook on High for 4 to 6 hours or until beans are tender.

3. Mash some of the beans to thicken mixture. Stir in tomatoes and olives. Cook for 20 to 30 minutes more, until thoroughly heated.

4. Ladle into bowls and sprinkle each with Parmesan cheese.

Non Pantry Staple Grocery List
2 cups dry great northern beans
1 cup sun-dried tomatoes
1 (2-oz.) can sliced black olives
¼ cup low-fat grated Parmesan cheese

Calories 114
Fat 3 g
Saturated Fat 1 g
Cholesterol 5 mg
Sodium 322 mg
Total Carbs 25 g
Fiber 8 g
Protein 8 g

Thyme Roasted Sweet Potatoes

Hope Comerford
Clinton Township, MI

Makes 6 servings
Prep. Time: 20 minutes ✿ Cooking Time: 7 hours ✿ Ideal slow-cooker size: 4-qt.

4–6 medium sweet potatoes, peeled, cubed

3 tablespoons olive oil

5–6 large garlic cloves, minced

⅓ cup fresh thyme leaves

½ teaspoon kosher salt

¼ teaspoon red pepper flakes

1. Place all ingredients into the crock and stir.

2. Cover and cook on Low for 7 hours, or until potatoes are tender.

Non Pantry Staple Grocery List
4–6 medium sweet potatoes
⅓ cup fresh thyme leaves

Calories 181
Fat 7 g
Saturated Fat 1 g
Cholesterol 0 mg
Sodium 233 mg
Total Carbs 28 g
Fiber 4 g
Protein 2 g

Honey Roasted Parsnips, Sweet Potatoes, and Apples

Gloria Yurkiewicz
Washington Boro, PA

Makes 4 servings
Prep. Time: 20 minutes & Cooking Time: 5 hours & Ideal slow-cooker size: 3-qt.

1½ cups parsnips, peeled and cubed

1 large sweet potato, peeled and cubed

2 firm red apples, cored and sliced thick

1 tablespoon olive oil

1 tablespoon honey

2 tablespoons liquid aminos

¼ teaspoon ground ginger

1. Mix parsnips, sweet potato, and apples in greased crock, tossed with all of the remaining ingredients.

2. Cover and cook on Low for 5 hours, or until parsnips and potato are tender when poked with a fork.

Non Pantry Staple Grocery List
1½ cups parsnips
1 large sweet potato
2 firm red apples
2 tablespoons liquid aminos

Calories 159
Fat 4 g
Saturated Fat 0.5 g
Cholesterol 0 mg
Sodium 356 mg
Total Carbs 33 g
Fiber 6 g
Protein 2 g

Roasted Butternut Squash

Marilyn Mowry
Irving, TX

Makes 15–20 servings
Prep. Time: 1 hour & Cooking Time: 4–6 hours & Ideal slow-cooker size: 6-qt.

¼ cup olive oil

2 teaspoons ground cinnamon, divided

½ teaspoon ground cumin

1¾ teaspoons salt, divided

5-lb. butternut squash, split in quarters and seeds removed

2 carrots, diced

1 large white onion, diced

2 Granny Smith apples, peeled, cored, and quartered

4 chipotles in adobo sauce, seeds scraped out, chopped

Roughly 10 cups vegetable stock

1. Mix olive oil, 1 teaspoon cinnamon, ground cumin and ¾ teaspoon salt in mixing bowl. Brush over the flesh of the quartered squash.

2. Place squash cut-side down on a rimmed baking sheet lined with foil.

3. Add carrots, onion, and apples to bowl with oil and toss. Spread on another foil-lined sheet.

4. Roast both trays for 40 to 50 minutes at 425°F until squash is soft and onion mix is golden brown. Scoop out the squash.

5. Put squash, veggie mix, chipotles, 1 teaspoon salt, and 1 teaspoon cinnamon in slow cooker. Add vegetable stock.

6. Cover and cook on High for 4 hours or on Low for 6 hours. Mash with a potato masher or puree with immersion blender.

Non Pantry Staple Grocery List
5-lb. butternut squash
2 carrots
2 Granny Smith apples
4 chipotles in adobo sauce

Calories 109
Fat 3 g
Saturated Fat 1 g
Cholesterol 0 mg
Sodium 397 mg
Total Carbs 17 g
Fiber 3 g
Protein 4 g

Hummus

Colleen Heatwole
Burton, MI

Makes 8 servings
Prep. Time: 15 minutes   &   Cooking Time: 40 minutes   &   Setting: Manual or Bean
Pressure: High   &   Release: Natural

1 cup dry chickpeas

4 cups water

2 tablespoons fresh lemon juice

¼ cup chopped onion

3 cloves garlic, minced

½ cup tahini (sesame paste)

2 teaspoons olive oil

2 teaspoons cumin

Pinch cayenne pepper

½ teaspoon salt

½ cup reserved chickpea cooking liquid

1. Place chickpeas and 4 cups water into inner pot of Instant Pot. Secure lid and make sure vent is set to sealing.

2. Cook chickpeas and water for 40 minutes using the manual high-pressure setting.

3. When cooking time is up, let the pressure release naturally.

4. Test the chickpeas. If still firm, cook using slow-cooker function until they are soft.

5. Drain the chickpeas, but save ½ cup of the cooking liquid.

6. Combine the chickpeas, lemon juice, onion, garlic, tahini, oil, cumin, pepper, and salt in a blender or food processor.

7. Puree until smooth, adding chickpea liquid as needed to thin the puree. Taste and adjust seasonings accordingly.

Non Pantry Staple Grocery List
1 cup dry chickpeas
2 tablespoons fresh lemon juice
½ cup tahini

Calories 200
Fat 11 g
Saturated Fat 1 g
Cholesterol 0 mg
Sodium 137 mg
Total Carbs 20 g
Fiber 4 g
Protein 8 g

Beans 'n Greens

Teri Sparks
Glen Burnie, MD

Makes 10 servings
Prep. Time: 30 minutes ♣ *Cooking Time: 6–8 hours* ♣ *Ideal slow-cooker size: 4- or 5-qt.*

1 lb. dry 13-bean mix

5 cups vegetable broth

¼ cup chopped scallions

½ teaspoon black pepper

2 tablespoons dried parsley

1 yellow onion, coarsely chopped

3 cloves garlic, chopped

1 tablespoon olive oil

6 cups fresh kale, torn into 2-inch pieces

Plain nonfat Greek yogurt or sour cream, optional

1. Rinse and place beans in 4-qt. slow cooker.

2. Add broth, scallions, pepper, and parsley.

3. In skillet, sauté yellow onion and garlic in oil. Add to beans in slow cooker.

4. Pile kale on top of bean mixture and cover with lid (crock will be very full).

5. Cook on High for 1 hour. Greens will have wilted some, so stir to combine all ingredients. Replace lid.

6. Cook on Low for 6 to 8 hours.

7. Top individual servings with dollops of Greek yogurt if you wish.

Non Pantry Staple Grocery List
1 lb. dry 13-bean mix
¼ cup chopped scallions
6 cups fresh kale
Plain nonfat Greek yogurt or sour
   cream, optional

Calories 111
Fat 2 g
Saturated Fat 0 g
Cholesterol 0 mg
Sodium 182 mg
Total Carbs 19 g
Fiber 7 g
Protein 6 g

Lentils and Barley

Linda Yoder
Fresno, OH

Makes 3–4 servings
Prep. Time: 5 minutes & *Cooking Time: 3–4 hours* & *Ideal slow-cooker size: 3-qt.*

3 cups vegetable broth

I cup uncooked lentils, rinsed and drained

3 tablespoons olive oil

½ cup uncooked barley, rolled or pearl

I large onion, chopped

I clove garlic, minced

¼ lb. fresh mushrooms, cleaned and sliced, optional

I tablespoon Worcestershire sauce

I teaspoon dried thyme

⅛ teaspoon ground pepper

Salt to taste

2 tablespoons chopped fresh parsley

Extra-virgin olive oil for garnish

1. Place all ingredients into the crock and stir.

2. Cover and cook on Low for 3 to 4 hours.

TIPS

1. If using pearl barley, you may need to increase the cooking time by 30 to 60 more minutes.

2. The olive oil garnish is the "frosting on the cake" for this recipe.

Non Pantry Staple Grocery List

I cup lentils

½ cup barley

¼ lb. fresh mushrooms

I tablespoon Worcestershire sauce

2 tablespoons chopped fresh parsley

Calories 378

Fat 11 g

Saturated Fat 2 g

Cholesterol 0 mg

Sodium 297 mg

Total Carbs 56 g

Fiber 10 g

Protein 16 g

Beans & Rice

Kris Zimmerman
Lititz, PA

Makes 6–8 servings
Prep. Time: 15 minutes ⚬ *Cooking Time: 2–3 hours* ⚬ *Ideal slow-cooker size: 3-qt.*

3 cups cooked beans of your choice,
rinsed and drained

1 cup brown rice

1 (14½-oz.) can diced tomatoes

1 tablespoon olive oil, melted

Salt to taste

1 teaspoon cumin

½ teaspoon garlic powder

2 cups water

Diced green chilies, optional

Hot sauce or cayenne pepper, optional

1. Place all ingredients in slow cooker and stir well.

2. Cover and cook on High for 2 to 3 hours. Begin checking at 2 to 2 ½ hours to see if your rice is done.

Non Pantry Staple Grocery List

3 cups cooked beans of your
choice

1 cup brown rice

1 (14½-oz.) can diced tomatoes

Diced green chilies, optional

Hot sauce, optional

Calories 209
Fat 3 g
Saturated Fat 0.5 g
Cholesterol 0 mg
Sodium 88 mg
Total Carbs 38 g
Fiber 8 g
Protein 8 g

Best Brown Rice

Colleen Heatwole
Burton, MI

Makes 6–12 servings
Prep. Time: 5 minutes ⚬ Cooking Time: 22 minutes ⚬ Setting: Manual
Pressure: High ⚬ Release: Natural then Manual

2 cups brown rice
2½ cups water

1. Rinse brown rice in a fine-mesh strainer.

2. Add rice and water to the inner pot of the Instant Pot.

3. Secure the lid and make sure vent is on sealing.

4. Use manual setting and select 22 minutes cooking time on High.

5. When cooking time is done, let the pressure release naturally for 10 minutes, then press cancel and manually release any remaining pressure.

Non Pantry Staple Grocery List
2 cups brown rice

Calories 113
Fat 1 g
Saturated Fat 0 g
Cholesterol 0 mg
Sodium 3 mg
Total Carbs 23 g
Fiber 1 g
Protein 2 g

Savory Rice

Jane Geigley
Lancaster, PA

Makes 6–8 servings
Prep. Time: 10 minutes   ❧   Cooking Time: 2–3 hours   ❧   Ideal slow-cooker size: 4-qt.

2 cups uncooked short-grain brown rice

5 cups water

1 tablespoon olive oil

½ teaspoon ground thyme

2 tablespoons dried parsley

2 teaspoons garlic powder

1 teaspoon dried basil

1 teaspoon salt

1. Mix rice, water, olive oil, thyme, parsley, garlic powder, basil, and salt.

2. Pour into slow cooker. Cover.

3. Cook on High for 2 to 3 hours or until water is absorbed.

Non Pantry Staple Grocery List
2 cups short-grain brown rice

Calories 190
Fat 3 g
Saturated Fat 0.5 g
Cholesterol 0 mg
Sodium 246 mg
Total Carbs 37 g
Fiber 2 g
Protein 4 g

Rice Guiso

Cynthia Hockman-Chupp
Canby, OR

Makes 3–6 servings
Prep. Time: 5 minutes ❧ Cooking Time: 15 minutes ❧ Setting: Rice
Pressure: High ❧ Release: Natural or Manual

1 tablespoon olive oil

1 onion, chopped

1 cup brown rice

1 teaspoon salt

⅛ teaspoon pepper

½ cup chopped bell pepper, any color
(or a variety of colors!)

1–1⅛ cups water

2 tablespoons tomato paste

1. Place all ingredients in inner pot of the Instant Pot. Stir.

2. Secure the lid and make sure vent is at sealing. Push rice button and set for 15 minutes. Allow to cook.

3. Use manual release for a final product that's more moist. Natural release for a slightly drier rice. I prefer natural release for this rice.

Non Pantry Staple Grocery List
1 cup brown rice
½ cup chopped bell pepper
(colors of your choice)
2 tablespoons tomato paste

Calories 145
Fat 3 g
Saturated Fat 0.5 g
Cholesterol 0 mg
Sodium 366 mg
Total Carbs 26 g
Fiber 2 g
Protein 3 g

Quinoa and Black Beans

Gloria Frey
Lebanon, PA

Makes 6–8 servings
Prep. Time: 15 minutes ♣ Cooking Time: 2–3 hours ♣ Ideal slow-cooker size: 4-qt.

1 onion, chopped

3 cloves garlic, chopped

1 red bell pepper, chopped

1 teaspoon olive oil

¾ cup uncooked quinoa

1½ cups vegetable broth

1 teaspoon ground cumin

¼ teaspoon cayenne pepper

Salt and pepper to taste

1 cup frozen corn

2 (15-oz.) cans black beans, rinsed and drained

½ cup fresh cilantro, chopped

1. Sauté onion, garlic, and red bell pepper in olive oil in skillet until softened. Place in 4-qt. slow cooker.

2. Mix quinoa into the vegetables and cover with vegetable broth.

3. Season with cumin, cayenne pepper, salt, and pepper.

4. Cover. Cook on Low for 1 to 2 hours until quinoa is done.

5. Stir frozen corn, beans, and cilantro into cooker and continue to cook on Low for 30 to 60 minutes until heated through.

Non Pantry Staple Grocery List
1 red bell pepper
¾ cup uncooked quinoa
1 cup frozen corn
2 (15-oz.) cans black beans
½ cup fresh cilantro

Calories 244
Fat 3 g
Saturated Fat 0.5 g
Cholesterol 0 mg
Sodium 66 mg
Total Carbs 43 g
Fiber 11 g
Protein 13 g

Quinoa with Almonds and Cranberries

Colleen Heatwole
Burton, MI

Makes 4 servings
Prep. Time: 5 minutes ॐ Cooking Time: 2 minutes ॐ Setting: Manual
Pressure: High ॐ Release: Natural then Manual

1 cup quinoa, rinsed well

½ cup roasted slivered almonds

1 vegetable bouillon cube

1½ cups water

¼ teaspoon salt, optional

1 cinnamon stick

½ cup dried cranberries or cherries

1 bay leaf

1. Add all ingredients to the inner pot of the Instant Pot.

2. Secure the lid and make sure vent is on sealing. Cook 2 minutes using high pressure in Manual Mode.

3. Turn off pot and let the pressure release naturally for 10 minutes. After 10 minutes are up, release pressure manually.

4. Remove cinnamon stick and bay leaf.

5. Fluff with fork and serve.

Non Pantry Staple Grocery List
1 cup quinoa
½ cup roasted slivered almonds
1 vegetable bouillon cube
1 cinnamon stick
½ cup dried cranberries or cherries

Calories 282
Fat 9 g
Saturated Fat 1 g
Cholesterol 0 mg
Sodium 365 mg
Total Carbs 43 g
Fiber 6 g
Protein 9 g

Cracked Wheat Pilaf

Carolyn Baer
Conrath, WI

Makes 4–6 servings
Prep. Time: 5 minutes ⚜ Cooking Time: 2 hours ⚜ Ideal slow-cooker size: 4-qt.

1 small onion, chopped

1 cup uncooked cracked wheat or bulgur

1 tablespoon olive oil

½ teaspoon salt

2 cups vegetable broth or stock

1. Sauté onion and wheat in oil, over medium heat, until onions are transparent and cracked wheat is glazed.

2. Pour into slow cooker. Add salt and broth.

3. Cook, covered, on Low for 2 hours or until liquid is absorbed.

Non Pantry Staple Grocery List
1 cup cracked wheat or bulgur

Calories 112
Fat 3 g
Saturated Fat 0 g
Cholesterol 0 mg
Sodium 274 mg
Total Carbs 21 g
Fiber 3 g
Protein 3 g

Israeli Couscous

Colleen Heatwole
Burton, MI

Makes 4–8 servings
Prep. Time: 5 minutes ⚕ Cooking Time: 5 minutes ⚕ Setting: Manual
Pressure: High ⚕ Release: Manual

2 tablespoons olive oil

1 (16-oz.) package Harvest Grains blend couscous (available at Trader Joe's and Amazon. If other couscous used, see adjustment of cooking time in directions.)

2½ cups vegetable broth

Salt and pepper to taste

1. Add olive oil to Instant Pot.

2. Add Harvest Grains Blend and vegetable broth and stir to combine.

3. Lock lid in place, make sure vent is at sealing, then use manual function and cook on High for 5 minutes. *If substituting a different brand of couscous, cook for one half of the recommended time listed on the package.

4. When time is up, do quick release.

5. Fluff with a fork and add salt and pepper to taste.

NOTE

While I hesitate to recommend brand-name items, I was exceedingly happy to be told about this recipe for Harvest Grains Blend. We don't live near Trader Joe's but I buy it there whenever I can. Harvest Grains Blend is truly a "savory blend of Israeli style couscous, orzo, baby garbanzo beans and red quinoa."

Non Pantry Staple Grocery List
1 (16-oz.) package Harvest Grains blend couscous

Calories 249
Fat 4 g
Saturated Fat 0.5 g
Cholesterol 0 mg
Sodium 108 mg
Total Carbs 45 g
Fiber 3 g
Protein 7 g

Herbed Rice and Lentil Casserole

Peg Zannotti
Tulsa, OK

Makes 4–6 servings
Prep. Time: 15 minutes ⚜ *Cooking Time: 4–6 hours* ⚜ *Ideal slow-cooker size: 4-qt.*

2⅔ cups vegetable broth, or water

¾ cup dried green lentils

¾ cup chopped onions

½ cup uncooked brown rice

¼ cup dry white wine or water

½ teaspoon dried basil

¼ teaspoon dried oregano

¼ teaspoon dried thyme

⅛ teaspoon garlic powder

½ cup low-fat shredded Italian-mix cheese or low-fat shredded cheddar cheese

1. Combine broth, lentils, onions, rice, wine, basil, oregano, thyme, garlic powder, and cheese.

2. Pour into 3-qt. slow cooker.

3. Cover.

4. Cook on Low for 4 to 6 hours, stirring once, until rice and lentils are tender.

Non Pantry Staple Grocery List
¾ cup green lentils
½ cup brown rice
¼ cup dry white wine
½ cup low-fat shredded Italian-mix cheese or cheddar cheese

Calories 360
Fat 24 g
Saturated Fat 3 g
Cholesterol 13 mg
Sodium 880 mg
Total Carbs 4 g
Fiber 0 g
Protein 28 g

Desserts

Chunky Applesauce

Hope Comerford
Clinton Township, MI

Makes 10 servings
Prep. Time: 20 minutes   Cooking Time: 6–8 hours   Ideal slow-cooker size: 3- or 4-qt.

3 lb. tart apples, peeled, cored, sliced

⅓ cup honey

½ cup water

1 teaspoon lemon zest

3 tablespoons lemon juice

3 cinnamon sticks

1. Spray the crock with nonstick spray.

2. Place all ingredients into the slow cooker. Stir to coat all apples.

3. Cover and cook on Low for 6 to 8 hours.

4. Remove cinnamon sticks and mash applesauce mixture lightly with a potato masher.

Non Pantry Staple Grocery List
3 lb. tart apples
1 lemon
3 cinnamon sticks

Calories 107
Fat 0 g
Saturated Fat 0 g
Cholesterol 0 mg
Sodium 3 mg
Total Carbs 29 g
Fiber 4 g
Protein 0.5 g

Baked Apples

Judy Gascho
Woodburn, OR

Makes 6 servings
Prep. Time: 15 minutes ⚶ Cooking Time: 9 minutes ⚶ Setting: Manual
Pressure: High ⚶ Release: Natural then Manual

6 medium apples, cored

1 cup no-sugar-added apple juice

¼ cup honey

¼ cup raisins or dried cranberries

1 teaspoon cinnamon

1. Put the apples into the inner pot of the Instant Pot.

2. Pour in the apple juice. Drizzle the honey over the apples, then sprinkle them with the raisins and cinnamon.

3. Close and lock the lid and be sure the steam vent is in the sealing position.

4. Cook for 9 minutes on Manual mode at high pressure.

5. When time is up, unplug and turn off the pressure cooker. Let pressure release naturally for 15 minutes, then manually release any remaining pressure.

6. Take off lid and remove apples to individual small bowls, adding cooking liquid to each.

Non Pantry Staple Grocery List
6 medium apples
1 cup no-sugar-added apple juice
½ cup raisins or dried cranberries

Calories 172
Fat 0 g
Saturated Fat 0 g
Cholesterol 0 mg
Sodium 4 mg
Total Carbs 39 g
Fiber 5 g
Protein 1 g

Baked Apples with Dates

Mary E. Wheatley
Mashpee, MA

Makes 8 servings
Prep. Time: 20–25 minutes ⚬ Cooking Time: 2–6 hours
Ideal slow-cooker size: 6-qt. oval, or large enough cooker that the apples can each sit on the floor of the cooker, rather than being stacked

8 medium baking apples
Filling:
¾ cup coarsely chopped dates
3 tablespoons chopped pecans
¼ cup honey
Topping:
1 teaspoon ground cinnamon
½ teaspoon ground nutmeg
1 tablespoon olive oil
½ cup water

1. Wash, core, and peel top third of apples.

2. Mix dates and chopped pecans with honey. Stuff into centers of apples where cores had been.

3. Set apples upright in slow cooker.

4. Sprinkle with cinnamon and nutmeg. Pour the olive oil evenly over each apple.

5. Add water around inside edge of cooker.

6. Cover. Cook on Low for 4 to 6 hours or on High for 2 to 3 hours, or until apples are as tender as you like them.

Non Pantry Staple Grocery List
8 medium baking apples
¾ cup chopped dates
3 tablespoons chopped pecans

Calories 234
Fat 6 g
Saturated Fat 1 g
Cholesterol 0 mg
Sodium 3 mg
Total Carbs 46 g
Fiber 7 g
Protein 2 g

Bananas Foster

Hope Comerford
Clinton Township, MI

Makes 6 servings
Prep. Time: 5–10 minutes ⚜ Cooking Time: 1½–2 hours ⚜ Ideal slow-cooker size: 4-qt.

1 tablespoon olive oil

3 tablespoons raw honey

3 tablespoons fresh lemon juice

¼ teaspoon cinnamon

Dash nutmeg

5 bananas (not green, but just yellow), sliced into ½-inch-thick slices

1. Combine the first five ingredients in the slow cooker.

2. Add the bananas and stir to coat them evenly.

3. Cover and cook on Low for 1½ to 2 hours.

Non Pantry Staple Grocery List
3 tablespoons fresh lemon juice
5 bananas

Calories 141
Fat 3 g
Saturated Fat 0.5 g
Cholesterol 0 mg
Sodium 2 mg
Total Carbs 32 g
Fiber 3 g
Protein 1 g

Dates in Cardamom Coffee Syrup

Margaret W. High
Lancaster, PA

Makes 12 servings

Prep. Time: 15 minutes ♣ *Cooking Time: 7–8 hours* ♣ *Ideal slow-cooker size: 3-qt.*

2 cups pitted, whole dried dates

2½ cups very strong, hot coffee

2 tablespoons honey

15 whole green cardamom pods

4-inch cinnamon stick

Plain nonfat Greek yogurt, for serving, optional

1. Combine dates, coffee, honey, cardamom, and cinnamon stick in slow cooker.

2. Cover and cook on High for 1 hour. Remove lid and continue to cook on High for 6 to 7 hours until sauce has reduced.

3. Pour dates and sauce into container and chill in fridge.

4. To serve, put a scoop of Greek yogurt in a small dish and add a few dates on top. Drizzle with a little sauce.

Non Pantry Staple Grocery List

2 cups pitted, whole dried dates

2½ cups very strong brewed coffee

15 whole green cardamom pods

4-inch cinnamon stick

Plain nonfat Greek yogurt, optional

Calories 118
Fat 0 g
Saturated Fat 0 g
Cholesterol 0 mg
Sodium 6 mg
Total Carbs 32 g
Fiber 3 g
Protein 1 g

Quick Yummy Peaches

Willard E. Roth
Elkhart, IN

Makes 6 servings
Prep. Time: 5–20 minutes ⚜ *Cooking Time: 5 hours* ⚜ *Ideal slow-cooker size: 3-qt.*

⅓ cup vegan baking mix
⅔ cup rolled oats
⅓ cup honey
1 teaspoon ground cinnamon
4 cups sliced fresh peaches
½ cup water

1. Mix baking mix, oats, honey, and cinnamon in greased slow cooker.

2. Stir in peaches and water.

3. Cook on Low for at least 5 hours. (If you like a drier cobbler, remove lid for the last 15 to 30 minutes of cooking.)

Non Pantry Staple Grocery List
⅓ cup vegan baking mix
⅔ cup rolled oats
4 cups sliced fresh peaches

Calories 221
Fat 2 g
Saturated Fat 0 g
Cholesterol 0 mg
Sodium 2 mg
Total Carbs 49 g
Fiber 5 g
Protein 5 g

Apple Cake

Sue Hamilton
Minooka, IL

Makes 8 servings
Prep. Time: 20 minutes ❧ *Cooking Time: 2½–3 hours* ❧ *Ideal slow-cooker size: 4-qt.*

1½ tablespoons ground flaxseed

4½ tablespoons water

1 cup whole wheat flour

2 teaspoons baking powder

1 teaspoon ground cinnamon

¼ teaspoon salt

4 medium cooking apples, chopped

¾ cup honey

2 teaspoons vanilla extract

1. Mix the flaxseed and water in a bowl and set aside to thicken for approximately 3 minutes.

2. Combine flour, baking powder, cinnamon, and salt.

3. Add apples, stirring lightly to coat.

4. Combine thickened flaxseed/water mixture, honey, and vanilla. Add to apple mixture. Stir until just moistened. Spoon into lightly greased slow cooker.

5. Cover. Bake on High for 2½ to 3 hours.

6. Serve warm.

Non Pantry Staple Grocery List

1½ tablespoons ground flaxseed

1 cup whole wheat flour

2 teaspoons baking powder

4 medium apples

2 teaspoons vanilla extract

Calories 207
Fat 1 g
Saturated Fat 0 g
Cholesterol 0 mg
Sodium 64 mg
Total Carbs 51 g
Fiber 4 g
Protein 3 g

Pineapple Bread Pudding

Janie Canupp
Millersville, MD

Makes 10 servings
Prep. Time: 15 minutes & Cooking Time: 2–3 hours & Ideal slow-cooker size: 4-qt.

3 tablespoons ground flaxseed

½ cup water plus 1 tablespoon water

2 tablespoons whole wheat flour

⅓ cup honey

2 cups chunked fresh pineapple and any juice you get from cutting it up

6 slices whole wheat bread

5⅓ tablespoons olive oil

1. Combine flaxseed and water in a bowl and let sit until thickened, approximately 3 minutes.

2. Mix flour and thickened flaxseed/water mixture until smooth. Stir in honey, pineapple, and juice. Set aside.

3. Break bread in small chunks and place in greased slow cooker.

4. Pour olive oil over bread.

5. Pour pineapple mixture over bread.

6. Cover and cook on Low for 2 to 3 hours, until brown and firm.

Non Pantry Staple Grocery List
3 tablespoons ground flaxseed
2 tablespoons whole wheat flour
2 cups chunked fresh pineapple
6 slices whole wheat bread

Calories 202
Fat 10 g
Saturated Fat 1.5 g
Cholesterol 0 mg
Sodium 178 mg
Total Carbs 28 g
Fiber 3 g
Protein 3 g

Fudgy Secret Brownies

Juanita Weaver
Johnsonville, IL

Makes 8 servings
Prep. Time: 10 minutes   ☙   Cooking Time: 1½–2 hours   ☙   Ideal slow-cooker size: 6- or 7-qt.

4 ounces unsweetened chocolate

¾ cup coconut oil

¾ cup frozen diced okra, partially thawed

6 ounces silken tofu

½ cup honey

1 teaspoon vanilla extract

¼ teaspoon salt

¾ cup coconut flour

½–¾ cup coarsely chopped walnuts or pecans, optional

1. Melt unsweetened chocolate and coconut oil in small saucepan.

2. Put okra and silken tofu in blender. Blend until smooth.

3. Combine all other ingredients in mixing bowl.

4. Pour melted chocolate and okra over the dry ingredients and stir with fork just until mixed.

5. Pour into greased slow cooker.

6. Cover and cook on High for 1½ to 2 hours.

Non Pantry Staple Grocery List

4 ounces unsweetened chocolate

¾ cup frozen diced okra

6 ounces silken tofu

1 teaspoon vanilla extract

¾ cup coconut flour

½–¾ cup coarsely chopped walnuts or pecans, optional

Calories 471
Fat 37 g
Saturated Fat 24 g
Cholesterol 0 mg
Sodium 231 mg
Total Carbs 29 g
Fiber 7 g
Protein 7 g

Black Bean Brownies

Juanita Weaver
Johnsonville, IL

Makes 6–8 servings
Prep. Time: 5 minutes ⚜ *Cooking Time: 1½ hours* ⚜ *Ideal slow-cooker size: 5- or 6-qt.*

1 (15-oz.) can black beans, rinsed and drained

12 ounces silken tofu

⅓ cup cocoa powder

1½ teaspoons aluminum-free baking powder

½ teaspoon baking soda

2 tablespoons coconut oil

2 teaspoons vanilla extract

⅓ cup plain nonfat Greek yogurt or low-fat cottage cheese

¼ cup honey

¼ teaspoon salt

1. Put all ingredients in a food processor or blender. Blend until smooth.

2. Pour into greased slow cooker.

3. Cover and cook for 1½ hours on High.

4. Cool in crock. For best taste, chill before serving.

Non Pantry Staple Grocery List

1 (15-oz.) can black beans

12 ounces silken tofu

⅓ cup cocoa powder

½ teaspoon baking soda

2 teaspoons vanilla extract

⅓ cup plain nonfat Greek yogurt or low-fat cottage cheese

Calories 179
Fat 6 g
Saturated Fat 4 g
Cholesterol 1 mg
Sodium 273 mg
Total Carbs 26 g
Fiber 7 g
Protein 10 g

Coconut Rice Pudding

Hope Comerford
Clinton Township, MI

Makes 6 servings
Prep. Time: 5 minutes ⚬ *Cooking Time: 2–2½ hours* ⚬ *Ideal slow-cooker size: 5- or 6-qt.*

2½ cups coconut milk

1 (14-oz.) can light coconut milk

½ cup honey

1 cup Arborio rice

1 cinnamon stick

1 cup dried cranberries, optional

1. Spray crock with nonstick spray.

2. In crock, whisk together the coconut milk, light coconut milk, and honey.

3. Add the rice and cinnamon stick.

4. Cover and cook on Low for about 2 to 2½ hours, or until rice is tender and the pudding has thickened.

5. Remove cinnamon stick. If using cranberries, sprinkle on top of each bowl of Coconut Rice Pudding.

Non Pantry Staple Grocery List
2½ cups coconut milk
1 (14-oz.) can light coconut milk
1 cup Arborio rice
1 cinnamon stick
1 cup dried cranberries, optional

Calories 244
Fat 6 g
Saturated Fat 4 g
Cholesterol 0 mg
Sodium 87 mg
Total Carbs 74 g
Fiber 3 g
Protein 4 g

Homestyle Bread Pudding

Lizzie Weaver
Ephrata, PA

Makes 6 servings
Prep. Time: 10–15 minutes   ❧   Cooking Time: 2–3 hours
Ideal slow-cooker size: Large enough to hold your baking insert

1½ tablespoons ground flaxseed

4½ tablespoons plus ½ cup water, divided

2¼ cups nondairy milk

½ teaspoon ground cinnamon

¼ teaspoon salt

⅓ cup honey

1 teaspoon vanilla extract

2 cups 1-inch whole wheat bread cubes

½ cup raisins

1. Mix the flaxseed and 4½ tablespoons water in a bowl and set aside for approximately 3 minutes, to thicken.

2. Once flaxseed/water mixture has thickened, combine all ingredients except remaining water in bowl. Pour into slow-cooker baking insert. Cover baking insert. Place on metal rack (or rubber jar rings) in bottom of slow cooker.

3. Pour ½ cup hot water into cooker around outside of insert.

4. Cover slow cooker. Cook on High for 2 to 3 hours.

5. Serve pudding warm or cold.

Non Pantry Staple Grocery List

1½ tablespoons ground flaxseed

2¼ cups nondairy milk

1 teaspoon vanilla extract

2 cups 1-inch whole wheat bread cubes

½ cup raisins

Calories 200
Fat 4 g
Saturated Fat 0.5 g
Cholesterol 0 mg
Sodium 339 mg
Total Carbs 40 g
Fiber 3 g
Protein 1 g

Metric Equivalent Measurements

If you're accustomed to using metric measurements, I don't want you to be inconvenienced by the imperial measurements I use in this book.

Use this handy chart, too, to figure out the size of the slow cooker you'll need for each recipe.

Weight (Dry Ingredients)

1 oz		30 g
4 oz	¼ lb	120 g
8 oz	½ lb	240 g
12 oz	¾ lb	360 g
16 oz	1 lb	480 g
32 oz	2 lb	960 g

Slow-Cooker Sizes

1-quart	0.96 l
2-quart	1.92 l
3-quart	2.88 l
4-quart	3.84 l
5-quart	4.80 l
6-quart	5.76 l
7-quart	6.72 l
8-quart	7.68 l

Volume (Liquid Ingredients)

½ tsp.		2 ml
1 tsp.		5 ml
1 Tbsp.	½ fl oz	15 ml
2 Tbsp.	1 fl oz	30 ml
¼ cup	2 fl oz	60 ml
⅓ cup	3 fl oz	80 ml
½ cup	4 fl oz	120 ml
⅔ cup	5 fl oz	160 ml
¾ cup	6 fl oz	180 ml
1 cup	8 fl oz	240 ml
1 pt	16 fl oz	480 ml
1 qt	32 fl oz	960 ml

Length

¼ in	6 mm
½ in	13 mm
¾ in	19 mm
1 in	25 mm
6 in	15 cm
12 in	30 cm

Recipe & Ingredient Index

About the Author

Hope Comerford is a mom, wife, elementary music teacher, blogger, recipe developer, public speaker, Young Living Essential Oils essential oil enthusiast/educator, and published author. In 2013, she was diagnosed with a severe gluten intolerance and since then has spent many hours creating easy, practical, and delicious gluten-free recipes that can be enjoyed by both those who are affected by gluten and those who are not.

Growing up, Hope spent many hours in the kitchen with her Meme (grandmother), and her love for cooking grew from there. While working on her master's degree when her daughter was young, Hope turned to her slow cookers for some salvation and sanity. It was from there she began truly experimenting with recipes and quickly learned she had the ability to get a little more creative in the kitchen and develop her own recipes.

In 2010, Hope started her blog, *A Busy Mom's Slow Cooker Adventures*, to simply share the recipes she was making with her family and friends. She never imagined people all over the world would begin visiting her page and sharing her recipes with others as well. In 2013, Hope self-published her first cookbook, *Slow Cooker Recipes 10 Ingredients or Less and Gluten-Free*, and then later wrote *The Gluten-Free Slow Cooker*.

Hope became the new brand ambassador and author of Fix-It and Forget-It in mid-2016. Since then, she has brought her excitement and creativeness to the Fix-It and Forget-It brand. Through Fix-It and Forget-It, she has written *Fix-It and Forget-It Healthy Slow Cooker Cookbook*, *Fix-It and Forget-It Healthy 5-Ingredient Cookbook*, *Fix-It and Forget-It Instant Pot Cookbook*, *Fix-It and Forget-It Plant-Based Comfort Foods Cookbook*, *Fix-it and Forget-It Keto Plant-Based Cookbook*, and many more.

Hope lives in the city of Clinton Township, Michigan, near Metro Detroit. She has been happily married to her husband and best friend, Justin, since 2008. Together they have two children, Ella and Gavin, who are her motivation, inspiration, and heart. In her spare time, Hope enjoys traveling, singing, cooking, reading books, spending time with friends and family, and relaxing.